illinois terminal
In Color
VOLUME II

Northbound 302 at Virden 9-7-55

Southbound at Williamsville 5-2-53

featuring the photography of Eugene Van Dusen

by

William D. Volkmer

Copyright © 2001
Morning Sun Books, Inc.

All rights reserved. This book may not be reproduced in part or in whole without written permission from the publisher, except in the case of brief quotations or reproductions of the cover for the purposes of review.

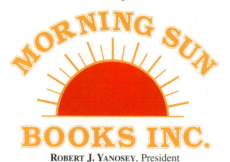

ROBERT J. YANOSEY, President
To access our full library *In Color* visit us at
www.morningsunbooks.com

Published by
Morning Sun Books, Inc.
9 Pheasant Lane
Scotch Plains, NJ 07076

Library of Congress
Catalog Card No. 98-065948

First Printing
ISBN 1-58248-057-5

Color separation and printing by
The Kutztown Publishing Co., Inc.
Kutztown, Pennsylvania

Acknowledgements

When Bob Yanosey asked me to help edit Gordon Lloyd's Morning Sun book on the Illinois Terminal, I had only a basic knowledge of the route, the cars, the infrastructure, etc. By the time I had finished editing and somewhat embellishing the text, I felt like I had actually ridden the line, which I am sorry to say I never had the chance to do. I studied the rosters, the photos, other texts on the subject etc. to the point where I felt I was, as they say in railroad lingo, "qualified over the railroad". At about the time Volume 1 of Illinois Terminal went to press, Bob handed over the entire Eugene Van Dusen slide collection and asked me to do a "Trackside" Edition featuring only Gene's collection. At that time, I felt like I had "OD'd" on the IT, but agreed to pursue the job. During my search for "new" material on the subject of the Illinois Terminal, my old friend Bob Townley introduced me to the absolutely unbelievable map collection drawn over a period of years by Mr. George Fehl of St. Louis. Bob loaned me his copy of the book, which is over two inches thick and contains every siding, every bridge, every tower, every junction, even down to the danger signs on the right-of-way and the type of catenary pole, and whether or not it had a concrete base. Mr. Fehl had walked over 480 miles of track with a sketch pad noting such things as the changing brick patterns on the station roof lines as an example. By drawing extensively from this work of art I was then able to pinpoint the exact locations of many of the photos. One example I like to point to is the case where the drawing of the Springfield station area notes that there is a mailbox on one of the catenary poles at the end of one of the tracks. On pulling a slide of the location, there it was, the mailbox on the pole just like the map said! Mr. Don Scott of St. Louis also furnished me various clippings and assorted other documentation. Factual information was drawn from *Trains Magazine* articles along with some printed material from the Illinois Traction Historical Society. There have been numerous rosters published over the years with some differences in facts as presented. Where roster information is presented here, it is hoped that the correct information is given. My sincere thanks go to Bob Yanosey, Bob Townley, Eugene Van Dusen, and Don Scott for their help in making this book possible. My thanks also go to Robert G. Lewis, Editor Emeritus of *Railway Age Magazine*, who loaned me a few pictures to make the story even more complete.

Eugene Van Dusen by this time needs no real introduction to the world of traction photographic history. Operating out of his home town of South Bend, Indiana, Gene or "Van" as many called him covered the gamut of traction lines, amassing probably one of the nation's finest and most complete photo collections on the subject. His work on the New York Central has already been featured in the Morning Sun book, *New York Central Trackside with Eugene Van Dusen*. Eighty-four years young at this writing, Van has been shooting color photos since 1934. All photography in this book, unless indicated otherwise, was taken by Eugene Van Dusen. Thank you, Gene, for preserving this history.

Gene Van Dusen and wife, Mary while on a bus trip to Hershey, PA in June, 2000.

TABLE OF CONTENTS

Named Cars on the Illinois Terminal Railroad 6	Peoria 60	Danville Power House 104
The Interurban at Work 7	Caldwell Hill 62	Roster Shots 105
The Interurban Station 8	Mackinaw Junction 63	The "Pull" Cars 111
Bridges and Trestles 20	Carlinville 65	Class B Motors 112
Steel Trestles 28	Morton 66	Class C Motors 113
Highway Overcrossings 30	Mindale 68	Class D Motors 114
Decatur Belt LIne 31	Springfield Area 69	Hybrid Electric Locomotives 115
Danville to Champaign 32	St. Louis Area 70	Work Equipment 116
Champaign Power Plant 39	The Illinois Side of the Mississippi .73	Freight Cars 117
Bloomington Power Plant 39	Alton Line 74	The Diesel Era 118
Champaign 40	Alton 78	IT Cars in Museums 120
Cerro Gordo 43	Granite City Local Service 81	Ohio Railway Museum 121
Decatur to Springfield 46	Studying the Streamliners 84	Fantrips 122
The Bloomington Line 48	Freight Service - The Main Line . . .94	Last Run to Danville 124
The Forsythe Shuttle 55	Gillespie Interlude 95	The Illinois Terminal Re-incarnated 125
	Freight to Danville 103	Final Frame 128

ILLINOIS TERMINAL In Color
VOLUME II

RAILROAD ILLINOIS TERMINAL COMPANY

Operating a railroad or a traction system requires the fine meshing of three basic departments. While there are indeed many departments that comprise a transportation entity, the three most important from a policy standpoint, are the Operating Department, the Mechanical Department and the Marketing Department. Departments such as track and signal maintenance, bridges and buildings, communications, power system, etc. are all very important functions, but they in themselves do not define the railroad, they merely support it.

Taking a closer look at the 'big three", the Marketing Department determines what kind of service and equipment is needed to satisfy the customers. The Mechanical Department either builds or purchases the required rolling stock to meet the demands set up by the Marketing Department. And finally, the Operating Department is required to operate the equipment in a safe and courteous manner to meet the demands of the customers that were attracted by the Marketing Department. The Operating Department is obviously constrained by the types and design of the rolling stock provided by the Mechanical Department.

In today's "throw away" world, railroads and transit authorities still function according to these time-honored rules, but with practices quite different from those of the interurban companies of the early part of the century, which is the subject of this book.

In recent years, it has been the practice that when a particular vehicle, be it a locomotive, a coach, a bus, an airplane etc., becomes obsolete, it is merely eliminated from the roster, scrapped, or sold to Mexico. A brand new state-of-the-art vehicle takes its place.

Not so with the Illinois Terminal Railroad. The Mechanical Department of that railroad was undeniably one of the most resourceful of any railroad, before or since, its existence. The IT never threw away anything! Virtually every last interurban car and locomotive to grace the IT roster was reused, rebuilt, remodeled, upgraded, reupholstered, and repainted, not once, but several times throughout its existence. If a car was retired into work car service or wrecked and retired, the motors and other usable parts were placed under unmotored trailers in order to continue their life.

When the IT needed more powerful locomotives, they used older locomotives, ballasted them and added more powerful motors.

The IT Marketing Department, ever competitive with paralleling steam railroads, was always searching for ways to draw more customers. They tried buffet meals literally from opening day, June 4, 1906 between Springfield and Granite City, which was the southern end of the line at that time. In 1909 they tried Party Cars, and in 1911 they began Parlor Car service. Reserved seat coaches came in 1914. Several seating change schemes resulted in the 1924 chair car program, dubbed the "Tangerine Flyers." Also, in 1911, IT gravitated to sleeping car service, a phenomenon that lasted three decades and included Bedroom Cars. Air-conditioning was introduced in the late 1920s and upgraded to mechanical type air-conditioning in the 1930s. Interior modernization was an ongoing process that involved the elimination of the classic leaded arch window glass that graced the IT interurban passenger cars and made them distinctive.

When the IT passenger Marketing Department made the decision in 1945 to once again modernize the fleet, for the first time since 1916, they chose to purchase NEW rolling stock. Even though eight new Streamlined cars were turned out of the St. Louis Car Company in 1948, the Decatur Shops continued to rebuild the old cars, turning out the Parlor Car *Cerro Gordo* to fill in, when the Streamliners were out of service for maintenance.

Thanks largely to the frugality of the Illinois Terminal and the ingenuity of its Mechanical forces over the years, the students of traction history were treated to a time-warp, of sorts, during the ten year period following the end of World War II.

Even after the various individual cars and locomotives were retired, the IT seldom scrapped them. Several of the class A and B locomotives went on to serve at power plants along the line. Trailers and sleepers were converted to Maintenance of Way Department bunk cars, locomotives were rebuilt to serve as snow plows, second hand C&LE freight motors were converted to demotored express trailers, some carbodies became yard offices and trainmen's rooms, and yes a couple of them became Instruction Cars. About the only time an IT car was scrapped was after it was demolished in a wreck or destroyed in a fire.

Alas, in 1949, the end of this time warp hovered into view and railfan photographers such as Eugene "Van" Van Dusen of South Bend, Indiana and Gordon E. Lloyd, of Chicago

The 273 southbound at the B&O interchange in Springfield 8-20-50

3

among others, made frequent visits to the "Land O' Corn" to record photographically, the end of an era.

Mr. Lloyd's coverage of the IT was chronicled in Volume I of this series.

Mr. Van Dusen's color photography work is illustrated here. Unfortunately, whereas Van had been shooting the IT in black and white for over 10 years prior to 1948, he began taking color slides just a very brief few years before the line was abandoned.

Whereas Volume I was geographically oriented, Volume II, presented here, will cover the same territory, but in a somewhat different manner. What we would like to do for at least a part of the book, is attempt to recreate scenes that we'd like to imagine could have existed in the early 1920s, when the interurban industry was in its heyday, but also a time in which color film had not yet been invented. At the same time we will attempt to identify the various interurban components, such as the stations, the bridges, the substations, and the cars, that all went into the make up of an interurban system in the early part of the 20th century. Hopefully, this presentation will in some way illustrate the slow, but steady changes that preceded the final abandonment of the Illinois Terminal Railroad electrified operation. As was shown in Volume I, the IT continued to carry freight with diesel power for another quarter century following the cessation of passenger service in 1958, largely through trackage rights agreements.

The name Illinois Terminal Railroad System came into general use in 1937 when an amalgamation of several complex components, referred to over the years by a host of names, leased roads, merged roads and so forth, the history of which is far beyond the scope of this book to unravel. Much of the material covered in this book was the product of a 1945 reorganization that resulted in the purchase of the eight lightweight streamlined cars plus the PCC cars.

ABOVE ● *The 277 southbound near East Peoria. April 19, 1952.*

RIGHT ● *The 277 and 276 on siding near Chatham. April 19, 1952.*

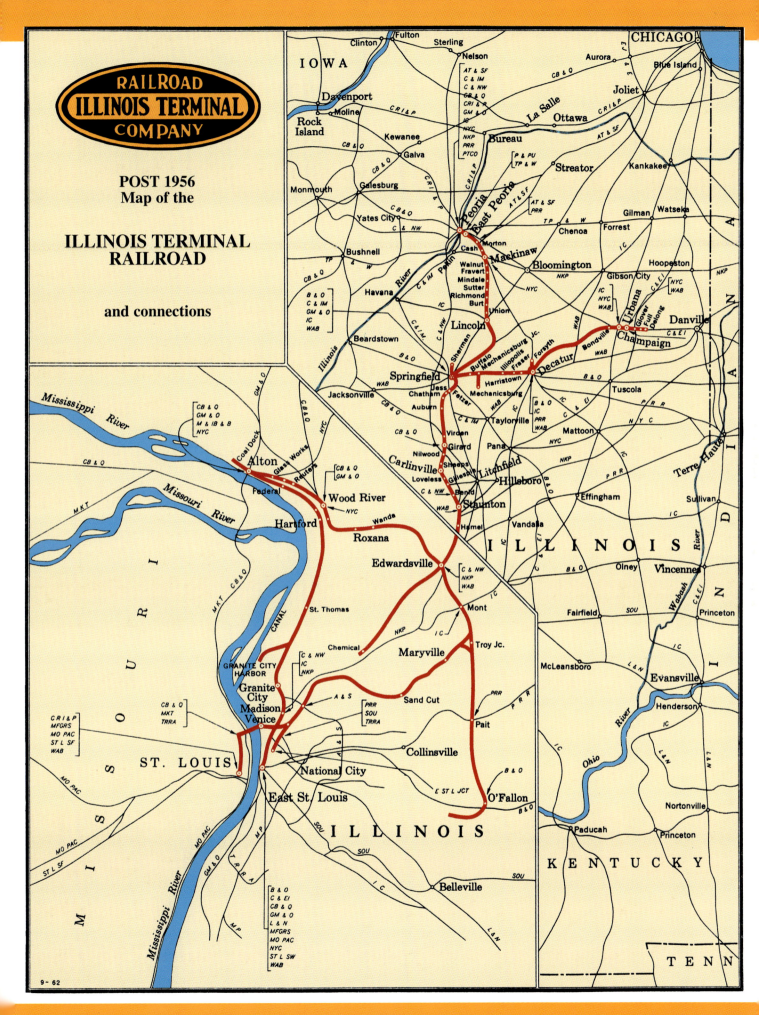

Named Cars on the Illinois Terminal Railroad

Car Name	Type	Year Built	Built By	Carried Name From-To	Became Number	Disposition
Champaign	open obs.	1906	Niles	1907-1909	270	Rebuilt to *Bloomington*
Peoria	Sleeper	1910	AC&F	1910-1938	049	Bunk Car/IERM
St. Louis	Sleeper	1910	AC&F	1910-1938	050	Bunk Car Scrapped 1938
Springfield	Sleeper	1911	Barney & Smith	1911-1938		Wrecked 1938
Decatur (I)	Sleeper	1903	Holland	1903-1911	272	Motor Car
Decatur (II)	Sleeper	1911	Barney & Smith	1911-1940	052	Bunk Car SFS 8-10-60
Edwardsville	Sleeper	1913	St. Louis	1913-1931		Burned 1931, SFS 9-30-33 (trailer)
Illinois-527	trailer	1911	St. Louis	1929-1942	535	
Homer	open obs.	1915	St. Louis	1915-1930	501/515/534	Became *Missouri (II)* 1930 became trailer 534 Scrapped 8-26-52
Louis Jolliet	Parlor Diner Obs.	1948	St. Louis	1948-1951	350	SFS 1962
Shadrach Bond	Parlor Diner Obs.	1948	St. Louis	1948-1951	351	SFS 1962
Pierre La Clede	Parlor Diner Obs.	1948	St. Louis	1948-1951	352	SFS 1962
Danville	Parlor	1906	Holland-CD&M	1907-1922	271	SFS 8-26-52
Bloomington	Combine	1906	Holland-CD&M	1909-1922	270	SFS 4-19-56
Champaign	Private	1906	Danville	1907-1927		Renamed *Sangamon* '27
Indiana	Private	1906	St. Louis	1906-1909	Converted to 258 4-09	SFS 11-13-50
Sangamon (ex- Champaign)	Party	1906	Danville	1927-1936		IERM 2-1-56 restored McKinley Private Car Scrapped 11-13-50
Monticello	Res. Seat Coach	1911	Danville	1911-1949	510 Remodeled in the late 1930's.	Scrapped 1949. Was trailer until 1926
Urbana	Res. Seat Coach	1911	Danville	1911-1950	511 Remodeled in the late 1930's.	Scrapped 1950
Cerro Gordo	Res. Seat Coach	1911	Danville	1911-1952	512 Remodeled in the late 1930's.	Scrapped 1952
Clinton	Res. Seat Coach	1911	Danville	1911-1950	513 Remodeled in the late 1930's.	Scrapped 1950
Lincoln	Res. Seat Coach	1911	Danville	1911-1940	514	Converted to bunk car 081 in 8-40
Granite City	Res. Seat Coach	1909	Danville	1911-1940	509	Scrapped 1940
Missouri (II)	Sleeper	1915	St. Louis	1930-?	515	Ex- *Homer*
Theodore	Sleeper	1903	Harlan & Hollingsworth	1903-1911		Ex- Demo
Francis	Sleeper	1903	Harlan & Hollingsworth	1903-1911		Ex- Demo
Missouri (I)	Private	1909	St. Louis	1909-1930	233 (II) Converted by ACF in 1909	Office Car Preserved. Retired 5-16-56
Illinois (I)		1904	St. Louis	1906-1909	Conv. to 259	Wrecked 5-31-28.

THE INTERURBAN AT WORK

While preparing the slides that illustrate this book, the thought occurred to me that several of these photos, while taken in the decade of the 1950s, could very well have been made in the era around World War I when the interurban industry was in its heyday. Of course there was no color film with which to take these scenes in 1918, so I thought it would be interesting to group those photos that depict the interurban as the institution it once was. That was in a day when roads were cumbersome, narrow, often unpaved, dangerous, and time consuming to drive on. Most folk that lived on the farms in central Illinois depended upon the Illinois Terminal for transporting their milk, their newspapers, bread and their purchases from stores in St. Louis, Decatur etc. as well as themselves as they went about their daily business. So here are some scenes that might have well have been taken in Yesteryear, but of course were not.

ABOVE • The date is March 22, 1953 and the Sunday newspapers are being off-loaded onto a small truck at the hamlet of Morton, Ill. The papers had been brought there from St. Louis on Northbound train 74, consisting of combine 283 and box trailer car 0606. The scene had been repeated every week for almost half a century.

ABOVE • Some 13.5 miles west of Danville, in the small town of Fithian, car 285 has passed over the various road crossings kicking up a cloud of dust. Auto and truck traffic has resumed criss-crossing the right of way in the dusty wake of the interurban car. It was a hot August 18, 1951 and the town's grain elevators would soon be working overtime with the influx of local freshly harvested corn.

The Monticello station was an excellent example of the many small town stations dotting the lines of the Illinois Terminal. Monticello was on the line between Decatur and Danville, and today is home to a small railroad museum. Back on August 18, 1951 westbound car 285 makes a stop there and will soon curve around the station and head south on its way out of town towards Springfield via Bement and Cerro Gordo.

THE INTERURBAN STATION

THE INTERURBAN STATION - A SMALL TOWN INSTITUTION

In every city, town, and hamlet that was served by the Illinois Terminal Railroad, there was a station building of some sort. In the large cities they were of impressive stone and masonry construction. More often than not, the stations in the smaller towns shared quarters with the local substation, with its whirring rotary converters, changing the AC power over to DC trolley power. The station was like an artery that served to infuse life into the town via the interurban line. Small isolated towns were often not served by the large steam railroads, and hence the people appreciated the frequent and indeed, much cleaner transportation afforded by the interurbans.

ABOVE • The 277 has arrived at the new station in East Peoria from Decatur, back to back with another motor car, in order to haul the railfans to Danville for the next day's special commemorating the discontinuance of service to that city. The date was April 19, 1952, and no one at that time knew for sure that the 277 would someday be preserved at the Illinois Railway Museum in Union, Ill.

RIGHT • The terminal at Springfield on the other hand was a fairly substantial affair. After February 23, 1933 it consisted of five stub-end tracks and an imposing building. All trains had to back in or back out and use the wye at the north end of the yard to head towards their ultimate destination. Trains went north to Peoria, east to Danville and south to St. Louis from the station. The photo shows the terminal as it appeared on October 6, 1950.

ABOVE • Many of the stations, particularly at junction points, shared their facilities with a substation, whereby the stationmaster could keep an eye on the rotary converters and other electrical paraphernalia that was located inside. One such facility was at Bement where westbound car 285 was seen on August 18, 1951. The car was enroute from Danville to Springfield during the waning days of service on that branch. Today even those baggage carts shown in the photo are sought after as collector's items!

ABOVE • On April 19, 1952 Van caught the 285 and 1203 at Decatur Station. The station is the building on the right. The 285 would continue on to Springfield after connecting passengers boarded the 1203 on the left for the trip to Bloomington. In doing so, the 1203 would "backtrack" about two miles towards Champaign before turning north on the Bloomington line at a place called North Junction.

ABOVE • The interurban station at Morton, located just south of E. Peoria, appears to be sharing space with the power company. The track leading off to the right fed a two track freight yard. The devices in the trolley wire were either a presence detector for the signal system or a headway recording device to indicate the passage of a regular service car. Unfortunately as detailed as the Fehl maps are, they do not indicate the presence or usage of these devices. Car 278 paused northbound on March 15, 1953 with a late model Chrysler parked at the station.

ABOVE • A southbound freight train lead by class C freight motor 1598 is coming in off of the Peoria main at Edwardsville and will enter the Belt Line trackage. The passenger station is on the left in this May 2, 1953 view.

ABOVE • A two-car southbound limited, one of the six daily trains running between E. Peoria and St. Louis, stops at Edwardsville station on May 2, 1953. Edwardsville more or less marked the entrance into the St. Louis area and freight trains were yarded there for distribution in the St. Louis terminal. The Belt Line departed the main line at this point and went in a southeasterly direction skirting Granite City on the east.

ABOVE • On April 20, 1952, a week prior to the discontinuance of through service from Danville to Decatur, an Illini Railroad Club farewell special stops at the Urbana station enroute back to its origination point in Danville. At this point, the IT had trackage rights over the Illinois Central and Wabash railroads as a result of the 1937 construction of a belt line to avoid streets in the two cities. Local streetcar service in the two cities was abandoned at about the same time. After April 28, 1952, the IT trains operated east of this point only to Watkins/Delong. They would continue that mode for another year. After April 26, 1953, the IT trains did not operate east of Champaign.

RIGHT • The Danville station marked the easternmost point that the Illinois Terminal reached during its illustrious career. Like most interurban stations in medium sized cities across America, it was reached by extensive city street running. Danville was one of the first cities to be linked to the outside world by the McKinley system interurban empire builders. The line first opened in 1903 as the Danville, Urbana and Champaign Railway and finally became a part of the Illinois Traction System on January 1, 1923. The train we see here 49 years later, was to become one of the last, as it was a railfan special consisting of cars 285 and 532 leaving Danville station on April 20, 1952. The station edifice can be seen behind the cars along with the turnouts to the station sidings where freight was off-loaded.

ABOVE • An express truck off-loads car 203 (formerly 1203) at the Champaign Station on a foggy morning, September 20, 1954. At that time, Champaign was the easternmost extremity of the rapidly truncating system. All passenger service to Champaign would be abandoned June 11, 1955 with the tracks being torn up after October 16, 1961, when dieselized freight service was diverted to paralleling railroads. A wye just east of the Champaign station allowed the single-ended interurban to turn around for the trip back to Springfield.

ABOVE ● Exactly two miles east of Champaign station lay Urbana Station, separated by a wye and some industrial sidings. The IT track between the two stations was closely paralleled on the north side by the Peoria and Eastern Railroad, a New York Central subsidiary. A noon departure eastbound on August 18, 1951, for Danville has the usual car, 285. Patronage over the line had drastically dwindled since the war's end, and this route would soon become history. The construction style of Urbana and Champaign stations was strikingly similar, because both were built around 1937, when the IT main line was diverted a distance of 5.5 miles over the Wabash Railroad through this area.

LEFT, TOP • September 7, 1955 was an overcast day when "vest pocket" streamliner 300 (a term coined by the late *Trains Magazine* editor, David P. Morgan) made a southbound stop at Girard, Ill. Being of brick (i.e. solid) construction, the building survives to the present day as a private dwelling, minus the track in the front yard, of course.

LEFT, BOTTOM • The wood frame station at Auburn, Ill. plays host to a lone passenger about to board southbound streamliner 300. The waiting room ostensibly offered ample shelter during the downpour that has just produced the small lake shown in the photo. The date, September 7, 1955 indicates that in about six months the trackage in this area will revert to diesel-powered, freight-only.

RIGHT • May 1944 Schedule

ABOVE • The absence of trolley wire and a switch point in the pavement seem to testify that the siding into the Carlinville freight station has been long out of service. On May 2, 1953, a northbound train makes the stop in front of the passenger station. At one time there was a three-track freight yard, plus a wye at this location. The wye track here apparently stemmed from the fact that when the service from Springfield southward began in 1905, Carlinville was the southernmost end of the line.

ABOVE • Clinton, Illinois was roughly the half-way point between Decatur and Bloomington. On entering town from the north, the IT tracks traversed a brick-paved Monroe Street, about six blocks north of the Illinois Central Railroad crossing. The IC had a huge station in Clinton, containing division offices as well as waiting room area. On October 18, 1952, Illinois Terminal car 1202 clattered to a halt at this non-descript one-story edifice a couple of blocks south of the IC. The building behind the Ford pickup is the passenger station. The two story building housed the IT offices and freight station. From the looks of the switch-point ahead of the car, the Clinton wye was little used during this era.

ABOVE • The brick and sandstone architecture shown here at Buffalo, Illinois was a sort of "rubber-stamp" design, commonly referred to as a "McKinley style" station. There were several throughout the system and contained the trademark pigeon-holes along the roof line providing ventilation for the substation equipment on the ground floor. Car 284 is westbound at the station on May 2, 1953. This station still serves as a town maintenance garage and photos can be seen in Volume I of this series, page 39.

ABOVE • A two car train of center door cars with 104 bringing up the rear awaits departure from the station in Alton, bound for St. Louis on June 18, 1948. Alton was the end of a suburban line that made a connection with a railbus to Grafton, a few miles north up the Mississippi River. Because the 600 volt power was trainlined between the cars, only the lead car needed to have its trolley pole against the overhead wire. This practice was not too common on other interurban properties operating multiple-unit equipment, principally because of the hazard of 600 volts being present while the pole has been pulled into the down position on the car.

LEFT • The extreme small end of the IT station spectrum is typified by this waiting shelter at Ogden, about 18 miles west of Danville. The regular Danville line car, 285 approaches the shelter eastbound on August 18, 1951. After the line was cut back from Danville to Watkins (three miles east of here) in the Spring of 1952, Ogden wye was used to turn the trains. They then operated backwards the three miles to Watkins pointed west.

BRIDGES AND TRESTLES

Some of the most scenic locations on the Illinois Terminal at which to photograph the interurban at work were on the many picturesque trestles and truss bridges that permeated the system. Of the four basic routes, the Danville to Springfield segment seemed to have the most interesting collection of bridges and trestles.

One of the reasons they were so interesting is that one could capture the essence of the interurban there without the modern trappings of billboards, autos, highways etc. cluttering the photo. The photos on these pages were all made between 1949 and 1955, but could well have been made some 40 years previous, with little difference in their appearance. See if you don't agree.

ABOVE AND BELOW • Just west of Danville, the IT line to Champaign/Decatur crossed the Vermillion River on a deck girder bridge. Here are two views taken on the occasion of a fantrip, Sunday April 20, 1952. This was to be the farewell trip over the line using cars 285 and 532. The view was taken at track level and does not describe the bridge construction very well. However, Van and some of the other riders climbed down to the river level to take the shot below which does capture the nature and flavor of the bridge. It is interesting to ponder the fact that possibly there were many train crew personnel who had operated interurbans over this bridge for forty years and only viewed it as seen in the photo above, completely oblivious to what the bridge might have looked like from river level below. They probably did not *care* much either as to how the bridge was constructed or what it looked like. The bridge maintainers and the railfans took on that responsibility!

ABOVE • On page 15 of Gordon Lloyd's *Illinois Terminal in Color, Volume 1*, there is a magnificent photo of car 263 crossing the Opossum Trot trestle west of Danville. Van was not as fortunate, weatherwise in shooting color at this location, but managed to catch a somewhat more distinctive car crossing the trestle in the opposite direction, eastbound. Headed towards Danville on May 27, 1950 was car 271, one of two cars originally built in an all-parlor configuration for the Columbus, Delaware and Marion Railway and arguably among the very longest interurban cars ever built. Oh yes, that's the Middle Fork River down below.

ABOVE • Eleven miles east of Champaign, car 276 rumbles across the timber pile trestle at St. Joseph, Ill. enroute to Danville on August 19, 1950. Cars painted blue and white were now becoming more common as the Decatur shops worked to modernize the old cars to make them resemble the newly acquired streamliners. The Streamliners that had ushered in the blue car era were now a year and a half old. Chasing the cars in regular service was tough, because they had the advantage of using a private right-of-way, and dwell times were extremely short in the towns that the IT served. The time is 10:24 AM and train 70 had left Champaign at 10:00. Twenty four minutes to cover 11 miles is averaging about 30 miles per hour. Not too bad considering the stops along the way.

RIGHT AND BELOW • Perhaps one of the most scenic overlooks on the entire Illinois Terminal system was situated on the south side of Lake Decatur near the city of the same name. The lake had been artificially created by construction of a dam on the Sangamon River. Van spent the afternoon of August 19, 1950 at this location, among others, chasing cars on the Decatur to Danville main. It was one of those hot summer afternoons where the clouds had built up such that the sun played peek-a-boo with the landscape. The eastbound car 285 happened to cross the bridge while the sun was behind a cloud, but the intrepid photographer's patience was rewarded by the sun coming out simultaneously with the passing of the westbound car, number 276.

LEFT • On what appears to have been a warm spring day, car 278 was the chartered car of the Illini Railroad Club out of East Peoria. The date was March 21, 1953 and the photo shoot was on a short girder bridge crossing over the Pennsylvania Railroad branch running into Peoria, a few miles to the north. The photo was taken from the shoulder of paralleling U.S. Rt. 150. IT diesels would use the PRR tracks under the bridge into E. Peoria following the discontinuance of passenger service, during the period from December 20, 1955 to July 30, 1966.

ABOVE • Those puffy white clouds are normally beautiful to look at, and are usually a photographer's delight. That is, unless you are a photographer of the railroad scene, and are waiting to shoot a passing train or interurban that happens to pass by during one of the moments that a cloud has rolled in front of the sun! Such was the case on August 18, 1951, when Mr. Van Dusen patiently awaited the passing of interurban car 263 as it approached the overpass over the Wabash Railroad at Bement. Bement is about 28 miles west of Champaign. The clouded over sun not withstanding, it is an interesting interurban photo nevertheless.

RIGHT • Gene was "getting his kicks on Route 66" on the morning of August 20, 1950 as northbound car 274 was arriving at the south side of Springfield. Actually this particular Art-Deco design bridge spanned 6th Street just south of the Springfield city limits. The run was train 82, due into Springfield at 7:25 AM.

RIGHT • Possibly the longest trestle on the entire IT system was this wooden work of art leading to the McKinley Bridge over the Mississippi River. It was known as the Venice High Line Bridge. By October 17, 1952, when this photo was made, a substantial number of the Alton line cars had been converted from orange to green paint. Even though the Alton cars operated through Granite City, the Granite City local cars did not use this trestle. Rather, they operated via Madison Ave. on surface streets to Granite City.

BELOW • Southbound train 85 left Springfield at 9:10 AM for St. Louis on August 20, 1950. It is crossing over state highways 36, 54, and 29 on its way out of town. By this time, the highways were winning and the interurban was losing in the great popularity contest of the time. Car 283 was doing the honors this day, to a less than sellout crowd!

ABOVE • A two-car railfan special posed at Venice, Ill. as they came down off the McKinley Bridge approach on May 3, 1953. Service frequency was being severely cut back during this time frame because of a steep decline in riding and the previous discontinuance of the Alton line service. This phenomenon was plaguing transportation companies nationwide, not just on the Illinois Terminal.

STEEL TRESTLES

In the vicinity of East St. Louis, the Illinois Terminal frequently was required to cross over large expanses of railroad freight yards in order to reach the Mississippi River crossing. On these pages a sampling of those crossings is presented. The preponderance of the bridges were steel trestle and through truss construction with the exception of the final long wooden trestle nearest the McKinley Bridge.

ABOVE • On the Alton line, a suburban operation out of St. Louis, passengers were treated to an aerial view of the Mitchell, Illinois yards from the windows of car 103, on October 6, 1950. The bridge was known as the McCambridge viaduct.

ABOVE • Two years later, on October 17, 1952, the same car, 103, is northbound crossing over the Illinois Central and the TRRA tracks in Madison, Ill. As was typical of interurban routings, there was a paralleling highway bridge to the right, offering competition in the form of private automobiles.

ABOVE • The eastern approach to the McKinley Bridge across the Mississippi is illustrated in this view showing battery electric motor number 52 lowering a string of freight cars down off of the bridge at Venice, IL on May 3, 1953. At that time the preponderance of U.S. freight cars were 40 footers, as is evident in this photo.

ABOVE • The majestic McKinley Bridge over the Mississippi River serves as a backdrop as we see PCC car 453 descending the Broadway incline into Venice, Ill on May 3, 1953. Chronologically the PCC was at the exact mid-point of its 10-year life expectancy at that time.

HIGHWAY OVERCROSSINGS

Bridgework over highways tended to be less elaborate affairs than river crossings, largely because there was no threat of flooding in the area. However, the bridge often had to be rebuilt as a result of ongoing highway widening projects.

ABOVE • One such rebuild because the highway was being improved was this overcrossing over Highway 4, north of Carlinville. The two-car train, a blue motor and an orange trailer were sighted on the overpass on October 6, 1950, headed towards Peoria.

BELOW • About 22 miles north of Edwardsville was a point called Worden, where the Illinois Terminal ducked under the New York Central tracks. In a rather unique juncture, the county put a road through the underpass, somewhat complicating the interurban passage through the area. A railfan special, with car 277 in the lead, made a photo stop at this point on May 3, 1953.

ABOVE ● At the western end of the Decatur Belt Line, the IT swung north under the Wabash Railroad and ran parallel to Van Dyke Street enroute to the Decatur passenger station. Photos of the opposite side of this underpass and taken from the overpass appear in Volume I of this series. Car 284 is eastbound here having passed under the Wabash on May 2, 1953.

DECATUR BELT LINE

In the early years of development of the Illinois Traction System, it became painfully evident that the increasing use of the city street trackage by freight trains was to become a severe problem. In 1909, the IT began construction of a belt line freight railroad around the northern edge of Decatur. Freight trains began bypassing Decatur in 1911, but by 1930 the city wanted the passenger interurbans off the streets as well, due to continually increasing auto traffic. A new passenger station was opened for service in 1931. Similar venues were built in Springfield, Champaign, and Urbana.

LEFT ● The Illinois Central Railroad also built an overpass over the Decatur Belt Line in order to speed up traffic on both roads. The Pennsylvania Railroad shared trackage rights over the IC at this point. It was known locally as the Harrison Street Subway and crossed under the IC's original Freeport - Cairo main line. Car 284 has departed eastbound from Decatur Station, heading for Champaign. A little over a half mile east of the station, the car ducks under the IC and, in another half mile, will pass the former site of North Junction, once the diversion point for trains to Bloomington and East Peoria. That line had been abandoned some two months previous, in February, leaving a lone shuttle car operating between Decatur and Forsythe. Even that shuttle car had been discontinued for a week when this photo was made on May 2, 1953.

DANVILLE TO CHAMPAIGN

The Danville line was arguably the very Genesis of the McKinley traction empire that ultimately would become the Illinois Traction System, one of the nation's largest interurban networks. It began with the opening of six miles of line from Danville to Westville, in October 1901 and the subsequent opening of the Danville, Urbana and Champaign in 1904 and 1905. After that segment was opened, several small branches radiating out of Danville were also constructed. The latter day interurban ride from Decatur to Danville was some 88 miles. Few interurban rides in North American approached this length. Two other notable lengthy interurban runs were the Chilliwak line in British Columbia and the Sacramento Northern line in California which had both been abandoned before 1950.

Danville was also home to the Danville Car Company, builder of many of the ITS' early interurban cars and electric locomotives.

ABOVE AND RIGHT • It is a beautiful sunny day, August 18, 1951, and Illinois Terminal car 285 is rounding the curve from West Main Street into Vermillion in downtown Danville, amidst a veritable sea of vintage automobiles. This intersection represents the village square and about one block south of this point the car will have completed its trip from Decatur, halting at the local interurban station. Prior to 1936 local streetcars passed by this location with great regularity. At this late date in the mid-20th century, this scene was a true anachronism, whereas two decades previous, it was a very common sight in many locales throughout the country. The photo taken earlier the same morning, depicts orange car 263 southbound on Vermillion Street, having just departed the interurban station seen just behind the car. The car is about to turn right so as to again head west towards Champaign, Danville, and ultimately, Springfield where connections could be made to Peoria and St. Louis.

TOP RIGHT • May 1944 Schedule

Illinois Terminal Railroad Company

READ DOWN EASTWARD — SPRINGFIELD—DECATUR—CHAMPAIGN—URBANA—DANVILLE — **READ UP WESTWARD**

No. 78 Local Daily	No. 76 Local Daily	No. 74 Local ★ Daily	No. 72 Local ★ Daily	No. 70 Local ★ Daily	No. 68 Local Daily	No. 66 Local Daily	MILES	TABLE No. 2 (April 27, 1941)	No. 69 Local Daily	No. 71 Local ★ Daily	No. 73 Local Daily	No. 75 Local ★ Daily	No. 77 Local ★ Daily	No. 79 Local ★ Daily
PM	PM	PM	AM	AM		AM			AM	AM	AM	PM	PM	PM
8 30	4 05	1 00	10 00	7 30		1 30	0.0	Lv....**Springfield**....Ar.	4 00	8 35	10 50	2 55	5 55	9 00
8 42	4 17	1 12	10 12	7 42		f 1 40	5.6	Lv......Riverton......Lv.	f 3 49	8 22	10 37	f 2 42	5 42	8 47
f 8 50	f 4 25	f 1 19	f10 19	f 7 49		f 1 47	10.4	Lv......Dawson......Lv.	f 3 42	f 8 14	f10 30	f 2 35	f 5 33	f 8 38
8 54	4 30	1 24	10 24	7 54	I	f 1 50	13.0	Lv......Buffalo......Lv.	f 3 38	8 10	10 26	2 30	5 30	8 35
f 8 58	f 4 34	f 1 29	f10 29	f 7 59	N	f 1 54	16.2	Lv......Lanesville......Lv.	f 3 34	f 8 06	f10 20	f 2 26	f 5 26	f 8 31
9 06	4 43	1 35	10 35	8 06	V	f 2 00	21.8	Lv......Illiopolis......Lv.	f 3 28	7 58	10 13	2 18	5 18	8 23
f 9 10	f 4 50	f 1 40	f10 40	f 8 12	E	f 2 04	25.8	Lv......Niantic......Lv.	f 3 23	f 7 53	f10 08	f 2 13	f 5 14	f 8 19
f 9 19	f 4 58	f 1 48	f10 48	f 8 19	S	f 2 09	30.3	Lv......Harristown......Lv.	f 3 18	f 7 46	f10 01	f 2 06	f 5 06	f 8 11
9 30	5 10	2 00	11 00	8 30	T	2 20	37.1	Ar....**Decatur**....Lv.	3 07	7 35	9 50	1 52	4 55	8 00
9 33	5 13	2 03	11 03	8 33	I	2 30	37.1	Lv....**Decatur**....Ar.	3 05	# 7 30	9 46	1 48	4 51	7 57
f 9 52	f 5 34	f 2 22	f11 21	f 8 51	N	f 2 47	47.5	Lv......Oakley......Lv.	f 2 47	f 7 09	f 9 25	f 1 27	f 4 32	f 7 39
9 57	5 40	2 28	11 26	8 57		f 2 51	51.6	Lv......Cerro Gordo......Lv.	f 2 42	7 04	9 20	1 22	4 27	7 34
f10 04	f 5 47	f 2 35	f11 32	f 9 03	A	f 2 57	55.8	Lv......Milmine......Lv.	f 2 35	f 6 57	f 9 13	f 1 15	f 4 20	f 7 27
10 11	5 54	2 42	11 39	9 10	M	3 04	60.2	Lv......Bement......Lv.	f 2 29	6 49	9 05	1 07	4 12	7 20
10 21	6 04	2 52	11 49	9 20	E	3 14	67.2	Lv......Monticello......Lv.	2 19	6 36	8 55	12 57	4 02	7 09
f10 30	f 6 15	f 3 01	f11 58	f 9 30	R	f 3 23	73.0	Lv......White Heath......Lv.	f 2 12	f 8 47	f12 48	f 3 53	f 7 00	
f10 38	f 6 23	f 3 09	f12 06	f 9 38	I	f 3 30	78.1	Lv......Seymour......Lv.	f 2 06	f 6 21	f 8 40	f12 41	f 3 46	f 6 53
f10 43	f 6 28	f 3 14	f12 11	f 9 42	C	f 3 34	80.6	Lv......Bondville......Lv.	f 2 02	f 6 16	f 8 35	f12 36	f 3 41	f 6 48
10 55	6 40	3 28	12 23	9 54	A	3 45	88.0	Ar....**Champaign**....Lv.	1 50	6 05	8 22	12 23	3 28	6 36
	6 40	3 28	12 23	9 54	5 55		88.0	Lv....**Champaign**....Ar.		8 22	12 23	3 28	6 36	10 05
	6 47	3 33	12 28	9 59	6 00		90.1	Lv......Urbana......Lv.		8 17	12 17	3 22	6 30	9 58
	7 06	3 49	12 46	10 16	6 17		98.9	Lv......St. Joseph......Lv.		8 01	12 01	3 06	6 13	9 41
	f 7 09	f 3 52	f12 50	f10 19	f 6 20		100.4	Lv......Glover......Lv.		f 7 58	f11 58	f 3 03	f 6 10	f 9 38
	f 7 14	f 3 57	f12 54	f10 24	f 6 25		103.5	Lv......Ogden......Lv.		f 7 53	f11 53	f 2 58	f 6 05	f 9 33
	f 7 21	f 4 04	f 1 02	f10 31	f 6 32		107.5	Lv......Fithian......Lv.		f 7 44	f11 44	f 2 49	f 5 56	f 9 24
	f 7 23	f 4 06	f 1 04	f10 33	f 6 34		109.4	Lv......Muncie......Lv.		f 7 42	f11 42	f 2 46	f 5 53	f 9 21
	f 7 27	f 4 10	f 1 07	f10 37	f 6 37		111.4	Lv......Bronson......Lv.		f 7 38	f11 38	f 2 43	f 5 49	f 9 18
	f 7 30	f 4 13	f 1 10	f10 40	f 6 40		113.0	Lv......Oakwood......Lv.		f 7 36	f11 36	f 2 41	f 5 47	f 9 16
	7 50	4 35	1 30	11 00	7 00		121.4	Ar......**Danville**......Lv.		7 20	11 20	2 25	5 30	9 00
	PM	PM	PM	AM	AM					AM	AM	PM	PM	PM

From the Office... or the Home — TELEPHONE YOUR TRAVEL REQUIREMENTS

BUY U. S. WAR BONDS and SAVINGS STAMPS

INVEST IN AMERICA'S VICTORY

Don't Worry About Your Baggage—Insure It

WESTERN UNION telegrams accepted on trains and at principal stations. Do not forget to telegraph the time of your arrival or to wire ahead for reservations.

RAILWAY EXPRESS SERVICE — Railway Express Agency Operates Express Service of the Illinois Terminal Railroad Company.—This Agency maintains a unified, nation-wide system for the expedited transportation of shipments. It offers a dependable service, augmented by through-car routes and special express trains, an alert organization of 57,000 trained expressmen for delivery and collection at all large cities and towns.

No. 81 Local Daily
PM
10 05
9 58
9 41
f 9 38
f 9 33
f 9 24
f 9 21
f 9 18
f 9 16
9 00
PM

ABOVE • The next morning, August 19, 1951 car 285 is seen leaving Danville, westbound to Champaign. The car is operating west on West Main Street. Whereas gas stations dotted the landscape, it is noteworthy that fast food establishments had yet to inundate the urban landscape. That phenomenon was still at least a dozen years into the future.

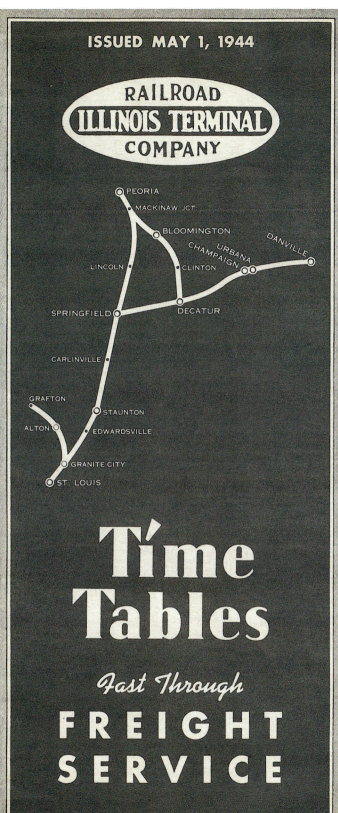

ABOVE • The scene taken late in the afternoon of August 18, 1951 could easily date back to August 18, 1921 owing to the absence of residential and industrial growth, let alone the absence of highway clutter. Car 263 is westbound, leaving Danville and was seen from a highway overpass vantage point allowing a panoramic view of the interurban infrastructure. Looking at this photo and knowing that it is mid-summer, one can almost smell the hot traction motors in the air!

RIGHT, TOP • Arriving at Danville the evening before a fantrip on August 19, 1950, Van found freight motor 1583 tied up for the weekend with a caboose. Freight was never a really important commodity on the Danville line largely because of the stiff competition from paralleling steam roads. The 1583 was the IT's eighth four-truck, eight-motor creation, and the only Class "C" loco to have been equipped with Westinghouse motors and controls. All of the rest of the class were General Electric equipped.

RIGHT, BOTTOM • Three and a half miles short of its Danville destination, eastbound car 285 has just finished crossing the Middle Fork River on the Possum Trot trestle. It is high noon on August 18, 1951.

ABOVE • 4.6 miles east of St. Joseph, the 276 is again caught up with and nailed whizzing along just west of Ogden, enroute to Danville.

ABOVE • Car 284 rounds a curve in the tiny village of St. Joseph, nine miles west of Champaign/Urbana. The track area has yet to be paved on April 25, 1953. That fact would make it less difficult for salvage crews to remove the tracks following the abandonment of the line.

CHAMPAIGN POWER PLANT

ABOVE • At about the same time that this photo was taken, September 9, 1951, General Douglas MacArthur was being quoted as saying, "Old soldiers never die, they just fade away." William McKinley, the Illinois Terminal President surely must have decreed, at some time or another that "Old freight motors must never die, they shall be retired to power plants!" Hence we have Illinois Power Company number 1, a former IT "soldier" living out its last days at the Champaign power plant.

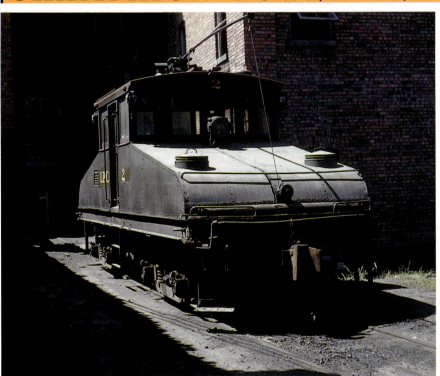

BLOOMINGTON POWER PLANT

LEFT • Illinois Iowa Power 2 was stationed at the Bloomington power plant, located just south of the Peoria and Eastern/NKP crossing in the center of town. The locomotive was photographed there on August 20, 1950.

CHAMPAIGN

ABOVE • Champaign had a small freight yard just east of the station, which during the latter years of operation served as part of a wye used to turn trains. The town was made the eastern end of passenger service following truncation of the line from Springfield to Danville. On September 18, 1954 car 202 (formerly 1202) was being turned on the wye at this location.

ABOVE • The photo shows the street located just behind the photographer in the scene above. A fantrip with car 276 on May 3, 1953 has pulled south into Neil Street prior to backing into the yard in order to make the turn-around.

ABOVE ● Bob Lewis was riding in the cab of an eastbound interurban car on a cold winter day in February 1955 as the stop at Bondville was made. A lone passenger destined for Champaign is about to board. Service on this line would end on June 11, 1955. *(Robert G. Lewis)*

ABOVE ● It is hay-fever season once again as the dandelions and roses are blooming en-mass on May 3, 1953. An Illini Railroad Club special rolls past Seymour. The interurbans always seemed to allow a commanding view of backyard America until, of course, they reached the main part of town where they traversed the main street.

ABOVE • Lark Siding was located between Bement and Monticello. It was 26 miles east of Decatur and 25 miles west of Champaign. For all intents and purposes, it was the midpoint of the line connecting these two major IT cities. Car 284 is headed to Danville on April 19, 1952, among the corn silos and grain elevator that personify Illinois as the "Land O Corn."

CERRO GORDO

ABOVE • The farewell railfan special of April 20, 1952, celebrating (?) the impending cutback of the Danville line to Watkins, Illinois, passes through the tiny town of Cerro Gordo. Cerro Gordo is about 13 miles east of Decatur.

ABOVE • The side view near the same spot portrays the crew enjoying the relative working ease of drawing fantrip duty this date. No schedules to keep, tickets to punch, crabby passengers, mail and express to offload etc. A piece of cake. However, the unemployment line loomed in the very near future!

ABOVE • On March 22, 1953, car 284 was seen clattering across the Illinois Central level crossing in Decatur near North Junction. Most of the railroad crossings on the IT Decatur Belt Line were "grade separated", but not this particular one because the IC line was a lightly traveled branch extending in a northeasterly direction to Monticello.

RIGHT • 285 is seen here westbound coming into Decatur, having just crossed the long bridge over Lake Decatur. Large fills such as this were once the hallmark of interurban construction, long before they became fashionable for highway construction. In most cases, the fills were made to allow smooth, level running for the company's freight trains, but in this instance it was, of course, to prevent flooding of the tracks.

ABOVE ● The rear of car 284 is seen, departing Decatur eastbound, along a litter-strewn right-of-way on March 22, 1953.

ABOVE ● A two car Illini Railroad Club special headed by car 276 stops by the substation/station in Illiopolis on May 3, 1953. Illiopolis gets its name by being the geographical center of the state.

DECATUR TO SPRINGFIELD

ABOVE • The tiny town of Buffalo appears to be almost deserted on May 2, 1953 as car 284 rolls westbound down the main street of town. The car has but 13 miles remaining to reach its final destination, Springfield. An astute observer will notice the presence of a front trolley pole on this single-ended car. These were put on in the Spring of 1952 for convenience after the Danville line was cut back to DeLong, because of the reverse move required to access a turning wye at Ogden.

ABOVE • The trestle over the Sangamon River was partially destroyed in a freight train derailment many years previous and in their haste to restore the line to operation, this hodge-podge of timber and deck girders resulted. Car 285 was crossing eastbound on May 2, 1953 when this photo was made.

LEFT • The sun disappeared just in time to wreck an otherwise supurb interurban photograph. The location is Riverton, Ill., the date May 2, 1953. Car 284 is westbound on a practically deserted street, only about six miles from Springfield.

LEFT • The evening newspapers are loaded aboard car 283 at Springfield in August 1950. An express trailer accompanies the car, probably a through car from St. Louis to E. Peoria. The car in the rear is more than likely a separate run, destined for either Decatur or St. Louis since all runs headed into and backed out of the stub-ended Springfield station.

BELOW • The weather was not terribly exciting on the February 1955 day that Bob Lewis rode the IT from Springfield to Champaign. The car du jour was the 203 and passenger loads were sparse as Bob grabbed a quick photo before boarding. *(Robert G. Lewis)*

THE BLOOMINGTON LINE

The 66 mile Illinois Terminal interurban line from Decatur to Mackinaw Junction, where it connected with the main line from Springfield to Peoria, resulted from a combination of two predecessor lines, the Peoria, Bloomington, and Champaign Traction Company, and the Chicago, Bloomington and Decatur. The latter line covered the 45 miles between Bloomington and Decatur. Trains operated between East Peoria and Decatur, via Bloomington, from July 4, 1906 up until February 21, 1953, when the service was abruptly halted and the rails at Mackinaw Junction were unceremoniously severed.

The city of Bloomington had a city streetcar system that was abandoned in the 1930s. In the late 1940s and early 1950s, the city presented itself as a sort of "time warp" preservation of a part of Americana that had largely vanished elsewhere by 1930. The photos on the following pages illustrate the rural nature of the line coupled with the small cities and towns located along the line.

LEFT, TOP • Train number 44 leaving Bloomington at 3:41 PM with car 281 is seen northbound to Peoria on the afternoon of August 20, 1950. The vantage point is an NKP railroad overpass. Because freight traffic over this particular IT line was scant, the roadbed was not kept on a par with, say, the Peoria-Springfield-St. Louis line. Through freight car traffic could not be handled over this line because of the tight curves encountered in the city streets of downtown Bloomington.

LEFT, BOTTOM • Earlier that same day, August 20, 1952, southbound train 45 rolled into Bloomington, on schedule, at 2:45 PM. The car is operating south on Madison Street, after negotiating several sharp curves in the downtown business district. Should an automobile driver make an error in judgment while in the company with one of these huge monsters, the auto was certain to lose the battle.

ABOVE • A few minutes later, the car rolls to a stop in front of the Bloomington passenger station. A small yard behind the photographer accommodated freight deliveries. When meets were necessary, northbound trains generally backed into the siding behind the station, while Decatur-bound trains remained in the street to do their business. Boarding and alighting passengers were few in number in August 1950, and red ink was lining the ledger books as a result. Car 282 for some reason sported an angular number board on the roof over the center window, similar to the Class "D" freight motors.

ABOVE • Moments later car 282 clatters across the Peoria and Eastern Railroad tracks enroute to Clinton and Decatur. The Conductor, having acted as a flagman, is seen reboarding the rear of the car. He will soon give the two-bell signal to the motorman to continue the journey south. The date is August 20, 1950. This point was about as far north as interchange freight cars could go in Bloomington. Standard freight car couplers could not negotiate the tight curves in the streets to the north.

ABOVE • Immediately south of Bloomington, on the line to Clinton and Decatur, lay Price Siding. Our photographer is riding the head end of car 1201 as it makes a meet with southbound 1203 at that location on April 17, 1952. The northbound car is taking the siding to allow the southbound unrestricted right-of-way. The Big Four (NYC) tracks are to the right of the interurban, also leading to Decatur.

LEFT • On the south side of Bloomington, we see northbound train 44 approaching town. The 282 is operating over center-of-the-street trackage on Lincoln Street alongside Evergreen Cemetery. Other than railfans shooting pictures of dying interurban cars in action, there appears to be little other activity at this location and time.

ABOVE • Clinton, Illinois was the halfway point between Bloomington and Decatur. The 1202 rolls south along the brick paved main street enroute to Decatur. The three 1200 series cars were the mainstays of the line during its last year of operation. This photo was taken October 18, 1952, a scant few months prior to abandonment.

ABOVE • A Pennsy overpass north of Maroa, Ill. on August 18, 1951 allows an unobstructed view of car 1201, southbound, entering the street operation through town. In the otherwise flat Prairie State, photographers welcomed the chance to get "above it all" for such a photograph. The car had previously operated over private right-of-way to a point near the top of the picture and shared the street from that point to the southern part of town.

THE FORSYTHE SHUTTLE

Following the February 21, 1953 abandonment of the Bloomington line, a six-mile segment remained in operation from Decatur northward to the town of Forsythe. The lack of a turning wye on which to turn the cars at that point required the use of double ended equipment. Double ended car 405 was brought in from Granite City to perform passenger duty there until April 2, 1953, when permission was received to drop the service. Diesel freight operation was continued so as to serve customers in the Forsythe area.

ABOVE • On March 7, 1953 the ex-Illinois Valley line car 405 loaded passengers at the Decatur station. The weather was not conducive to good color photography that day so Van made it a point to return, two weekends later as it turned out, and with good reason, the operation was to be extremely short lived.

ABOVE • On the next visit, car 405 was first encountered southbound nearing Decatur's North Junction, the connecting point with the Champaign line. The date was March 22, 1953, and only one week was remaining on the clock for the shuttle to operate.

ABOVE • By the time the shuttle car made its next run to Forsythe, the sun was out and a fine photographic record could be made of the car and its short lived venue, this time at the Forsythe station.

BELOW • Again, on March 22, 1953, the 405 is shown between runs with both poles pulled, north of the Forsythe station. This is very close to the point where the rails were severed a month previous, ending service to Bloomington and Peoria. The Phillips Petroleum oil storage plant on the left represented the reason that this short segment of the line had been retained. Diesel locomotives were found to be derailment prone in this area and electric locomotives had been re-instituted until the time that the necessary trackwork corrections could be made.

ABOVE • Word had gotten out that the Bloomington line was not to last much longer, so with the fall foliage at its peak on October 16, 1952, Van captured the 1202 rolling north through Forsythe, four months before the end. The car is on Elwood Street at Shaper, and the track leading to the right served the "Phillips 66" tank farm. This would later serve as the end of the "Forsythe Shuttle" after abandonment of through service.

LEFT • Repainting of the older interurban cars had already begun when this photo was made on August 19, 1950. However, 281 had not yet received this treatment as it rolled past North Junction on the east side of Decatur. The IT cars were originally painted a dark green color and were gradually repainted into "traction orange" in the early 1930s.

ABOVE • Having arrived at Decatur station from Bloomington at 9:43 AM on August 19, 1950, the 281 will leave at 10:30 AM for the return trip as Train 42.

ABOVE • Over on an adjacent stub end siding, we find a regular Bloomington line stalwart, number 1202 on standby as the protect car for the line. It will leave at 2:15 PM northbound for Bloomington as train 44 on August 19, 1950. The reason this car has to fill in on the schedule is because the next scheduled inbound from Bloomington will not be until 4:35 PM.

ABOVE • A rear view of the same car, up against the bumping post at the end of the siding exemplifies the single ended design of the 1202. The 1200s seldom pulled passenger trailers, but often pulled express cars loaded with freight and newspapers.

ABOVE • Unrepainted locomotive 1567, still in the old original green livery was westbound at Decatur station on April 19, 1952. In the distance the Bloomington car can be seen on the station siding, out of the way of the freight for the time being.

PEORIA

The Illinois Terminal purchased the Streamliner trains in 1948. On the first test run into Peoria on October 21, 1948, it was learned that the Streamliners would not clear the station superstructure in Peoria. This gave the railroad management an excuse to abandon service over the Illinois River Bridge into downtown Peoria and terminate all train service in East Peoria. Because Mr. Van Dusen did not begin taking color slides on the IT until just prior to this event, we have only one photo to display taken in Peoria.

ABOVE ● On August 1, 1948 former open-observation-platformed, reserved-seat trailer 513 is seen entering the Peoria carbarns with a lighted tail sign bringing up the rear. Originally named the *Clinton*, the 513 was built by St. Louis Car Company in 1911 as a trailer, but a 1928 rebuild made it into a motorized trailer, by adding two traction motors from one of the 260 series cars that was being scrapped. The car was again rebuilt in 1930 with new furniture, and the paint scheme changed from green to orange. The car was again rebuilt in 1936, having its open observation platform filled in. In 1948, little did anyone realize that with the advent of the Streamliners in early 1949, service to downtown Peoria would be abandoned, because the Streamliners did not "Play Well in Peoria!" Nevertheless, the 513 was sold for scrap on November 13, 1950.

ABOVE ● After service was pulled back to East Peoria, a small shop was erected to service the cars. Here we see car 1203 on April 19, 1952 inside the rather spartan building that served as a shop for the interurban cars and freight motors.

ABOVE ● Car 277 was photographed at East Peoria station on April 19, 1952, the day before a special railfan trip was to operated out of Danville at the opposite end of the system. She would operate as an extra south to Springfield where it would be teamed up with trailer 532 and sent east to Danville. The railfan entourage, including Eugene Van Dusen would accompany the car in order to ride the special run the next day.

ABOVE ● After East Peoria became the northernmost point reached by the IT, in late 1948, a loop was constructed along with a new passenger station. Car 273 has just cleared the entrance to that turning loop and is proceeding outbound towards Springfield on September 7, 1953. The bridge that the car is crossing goes over Farm Creek and the two stall enginehouse/carbarn can be seen in the background. The car would soon be climbing the four mile grade known as Caldwell Hill towards Mackinaw Junction.

CALDWELL HILL

RIGHT AND BELOW • Caldwell Hill was a grade that began literally at the yard limits of East Peoria yard and extended about four miles south to the crest of the grade at Caldwell Siding. Helper engines were assigned to heavy freights southbound, usually a class B motor. A Streamliner is seen ascending the Hill on March 21, 1953. This portion of the Illinois Terminal from Peoria to Bloomington was originally constructed for AC operation, but was soon thereafter converted to DC for compatibility with the remainder of the system. A year earlier, on April 19, 1952, a Streamliner kicks up the dust as it breezes downgrade past Kerfoot Siding, while coasting into East Peoria at high speed.

ILLINOIS 62 TERMINAL

MACKINAW JUNCTION

Mackinaw Junction was located 9 miles south of East Peoria at the point where the main line to St. Louis veered off to the right while the Bloomington line went straight ahead. There was a combination substation/passenger station nestled inside of a wye.

Most of the photos on these pages were taken during a railfan excursion held on March 21, 1953, about a month after the Bloomington line was severed just below the junction. The main line continued in service until electrification ended in 1956 and shortly after dieselization, the traffic through this area was diverted to paralleling railroads.

ABOVE • After descending a short grade, car 278 has passed through the truss bridge over the Mackinaw River, seen in the background, followed by a wooden trestle crossing the flood plain adjacent to the river. At the moment the shutter was snapped, the car had just passed over the switch to the Bloomington line and a short stretch of station platform that represented Mackinaw Junction. While the substation in the picture was still in operation on March 21, 1953, the Bloomington line was not. The track in the foreground lead to Springfield and St. Louis.

RIGHT • During the March 21, 1953 railfan excursion, car 278 has been turned on the wye track in back of the substation and backed into the remaining stub that once continued on east and south to Bloomington.

ABOVE AND BELOW • The 278 having been turned on the wye to point northward has now been pulled up alongside the station at Mackinaw Junction during the March 21, 1953 railfan excursion. The photo was taken a year earlier, on April 19, 1952 when regular service from Bloomington was still provided. Car 1203, one of the Bloomington regulars was photographed at the same spot.

CARLINVILLE

ABOVE • It was Spring planting time on May 2, 1953 when this two-car train zipped alongside the fields north of Carlinville, enroute to Springfield. Train 84 had left Carlinville at 3:02 PM, arriving in Springfield at 4:15. The entire 100.2-mile run from St. Louis to Springfield consumed 3 hours and 5 minutes. 185 minutes to cover 100 miles with 18 stops and lots of street running meant that there was plenty of 60 miles per hour action!

ABOVE • Later on the day of the fantrip, March 21, 1953, a northbound freight was observed at Mackinaw Junction. The fact that both poles are up would indicate that a set off is being made. There is an ample serving of vintage freight cars in the train. One curiosity about the class "C" freight motors was that three of the four trolley poles sported carbon insert shoes, while the fourth pole retained the old-fashioned trolley wheel. It is theorized that the wheeled pole was always used for backup switching moves.

MORTON

Morton, second only to Bloomington represented one of the great places in the U.S. to go and observe interurban action in the most nostalgic settings. The passenger cars toting trailers rumbled down the center of the city streets creating a true interurban atmosphere. However, much to the dislike of the local residents, huge multicar freight trains also broke the silence of the otherwise peaceful town. Following the discontinuance of electric powered trains, the town negotiated the freight trains off of the city streets and onto paralleling diesel railroads. The post 1955 history of the traffic reroutings in Morton could fill a small book in itself.

ABOVE AND BELOW • It is March 21, 1953 and we are stationed at the southern edge of Morton, waiting to catch some of the action. Streamliner 300, leading a two-car train enters the city street trackage from the south, bound for East Peoria. After it clears, a freight rumbles south to rattle a normally very quiet neighborhood. Diesel powered trains ceased to use Jefferson Ave. in Morton on December 19, 1955 in favor of yet another Belt Line operation.

ILLINOIS 66 TERMINAL

ABOVE • Car 278 has just clattered across three Santa Fe Railroad tracks in Morton and posed for a photo opportunity by its charter sponsors on March 21, 1953. The Santa Fe depot stood just to the left of the photo.

ABOVE • Were it not for the lone automobile lurking behind the power pole on the left, this photo showing IT car 277 towing an express trailer (also known as a "bread car") northbound on the north side of Morton could be timeless in nature. In actuality it was taken on March 21, 1953, but without the automobile, it could easily have been taken in 1923.

MINDALE

RIGHT • The 9.6 mile stretch of track between Union and Mindale represented the IT's "racetrack." It enjoyed the fastest running time on the entire Illinois Terminal System, 9 minutes for about 10 miles. Trains 92 and 93 made that time some three years before the Streamliners were built and placed into service. The 283 was crossing Kickapoo Creek bridge between Lincoln and Union, just south of the high speed stretch.

BELOW • After leaving Springfield whether northbound or eastbound, the IT trains to both East Peoria and Decatur shared the same trackage for a short distance to Starne Tower, a junction point where the Peoria-bound cars turned left, as car 274 is doing here on August 20, 1950. Photographer Van Dusen was standing high atop a Route 66 overpass about 7:30 AM looking south towards Springfield, down the IC main line. Starne controlled movements on the Wabash Railroad also crossing in the foreground. The Wabash was bound for Kansas City (and N&W ownership), the IC to St. Louis, and the IT to oblivion, albeit via N&W takeover, enroute.

SPRINGFIELD AREA

ABOVE • Cars in regular service coming into Springfield from the north and east passed Starne Tower and then paralleled the IC main a short distance before negotiating the crossover in the foreground of this photo and running "wrong main" before entering the Springfield station. On a railfan special movement, car 284 in this photo, shown here on September 7, 1953 is bypassing the station. It has just crossed over Grand Avenue, seen in the background.

RIGHT • A closeup photo of the 284 after it was berthed in the stub-ended Springfield station, again on September 7, 1953. The mailbox on the pole was shown on the George Fehl map of the area, indicating the depth of detail that those maps contained. That strange rectangular object on the inside of the motorman's windshield was an electric windshield-defrosting device, common on automobiles of the day.

ST. LOUIS AREA

The St. Louis terminal trackage was a below-street-level affair in the years following the 1931 opening of a station building on 12th Street in uptown St. Louis. Prior to that time, an all surface route extended westward from the McKinley Bridge, but, of course, no color photographic records were ever made of that operation.

Following the 1955 cessation of interurban service into St. Louis, local streetcars served Granite City until they too were abandoned on June 22, 1958, ending electrified streetcar operation in Illinois.

ABOVE • This view of the station trackage under the terminal building looks south in early morning sunlight. It was made on the morning of September 7, 1953 and shows a Granite City PCC laying over. The street above is 12th Street in St. Louis.

RIGHT, TOP • A two-car Alton Limited train lead by car 101 has just descended off of the elevated structure in St. Louis and is about to curve left onto 9th Street enroute to the subway terminal on October 5, 1950. The block signal to the left of the train serves as a reminder that the ITS prided itself in being entirely operated with block signal protection.

RIGHT, BOTTOM • There was only about a two-block segment of surface trackage on the St. Louis side of the Mississippi after the new terminal opened in 1931. This photo shows most of it. Car 277, fresh from the paint booth in Decatur Shops is doing the honors for a railfan special photo stop on April 20, 1952. The trailer behind the 277 is car 532. Lack of time seems to have prevented the shop crew from repainting the roof of the car. It is spotted just short of the exit from street-level operation to the depressed cut approaching the subterranean St. Louis terminal complex. The 277 ultimately became the very last car to haul revenue passengers, operating as train 92 out of St. Louis on March 12, 1956. It, of course, survives to this day preserved at the Illinois Railway Museum in Union, Illinois.

LEFT ● The sun is just about finished shining on October 5, 1950 as a two-car train of 470 series suburban cars coasts down the subway incline and into the St. Louis station complex. The train is inbound from Granite City and probably Alton beyond.

ABOVE ● A closer view of PCC car 454 inbound into the subway terminal in St. Louis in February 1955. The interurban trains into the terminal by this time were few and far between, but the local suburban cars such as this one from Granite City were still on a frequent headway. *(Robert G. Lewis)*

THE ILLINOIS SIDE OF THE MISSISSIPPI

ABOVE • This is a motorman's eye view of the planked-over cartway of the eastern approaches to the McKinley Bridge crossing of the Mississippi River. The track was originally on private right-of-way over the bridge but in later years was shared with auto traffic. The bridge was opened to trolleys in 1910 and traffic patterns were altered over the years. The arrangement as it existed on September 7, 1953 is depicted here. After the advent of the Streamliners in 1950, all interurban traffic went straight ahead over the Venice High Line bridge in the distance. This view is looking east towards Venice.

ABOVE AND BELOW • Prior to July 1, 1930, electric traction service to Alton was via the tracks of the Alton Light and Traction Company, and the tracks looped around the city hall in downtown Alton. Then in 1930, the Illinois Terminal Railroad leased the steam line, St. Louis and Alton, along with two steam roads, the 40-mile Alton and Eastern and the Alton Terminal. A connection was made between the existing electric line at Wood River and the paralleling steam railroad. Trolley wires were then strung to a depot south of City Hall where a connection was made with a rail bus that took passengers on to Grafton. In addition, the IT leased the O'Fallon Division of the East St. Louis and Suburban Railroad. The Illinois Terminal officially purchased the St. Louis and Alton Railway on December 27, 1940, about the dawn of the age of color photography, at least by railfan standards. The railbus operation to Grafton was covered in Volume I of this series. The 100-series Alton Limited cars, seen on these pages, were inherited in the 1930 purchase deal. Towards the end of operation northbound car 101 makes the stop at Mitchell before crossing the long Mitchell Viaduct in the background. The date was October 17, 1952. In an earlier view car 103 of the same series is seen October 6, 1950 threading across the long McCambridge viaduct at Mitchell, Ill. spanning several freight yards.

ALTON LINE

Alton and Granite City represented bedroom communities on the Illinois side of the Mississippi River from St. Louis. Naturally the heaviest patronage on the line originated at the closer-in Granite City, and the trains beyond there, to Alton were operated less frequently. Prior to the introduction of PCC cars, both services were provided by two-car trains of 100-series and 480-series center entrance cars. At times when one-car trains would suffice, cars in the low 400-series were offered.

Service to Alton was discontinued on March 7, 1953, about two weeks after the Bloomington line was abandoned.

ABOVE • These same center-door cars had been plying the Alton line since 1917 and continued to roll until the line was abandoned on March 7, 1953. The inherited St. Louis and Alton roster consisted of nine cars, three of which were built in 1917 and two built in 1924. Four that the SL&A received were built by the East St. Louis and Suburban Ry. in 1924. Car 101 still operates today at the Illinois Railway Museum at Union, Ill. After repainting to the lime green of the PCC era, car 101 is shown southbound on McCambridge Ave. in Madison, Ill., on October 17, 1952 about six months prior to abandonment of the Alton line.

ABOVE • Traveling north out of Granite City, the Alton trains followed the side of the road through Namoki. Car 121 is bringing up the rear of a two car train on October 17, 1952. Service to Alton was suspended in March of the following year.

ABOVE AND LEFT • A two-car train of multiple-unit St. Louis Car Company center entrance cars operates through Granite City on October 6, 1950, enroute to Alton. Cars 470-473 were built in 1924 very similar in design to the famous Pacific Electric "Hollywood" cars. They were originally numbered 70-73, but were renumbered in the 470's in February 1935. Car 472 of the same group is shown, passing the Granite City yard and shops complex on October 6, 1950.

ABOVE AND BELOW— Hartford was one of the many suburban locales that the Alton line cars served. The 103 was caught southbound on Hawthorne Ave. in Hartford on October 17, 1952. On the same day, our intrepid photographer caught the same car northbound at Wood River stop. Just beyond this point, the line veered off to the left over former steam road right-of-way to enter Alton.

ALTON

PRECEEDING PAGE, ABOVE AND BELOW • This series of three photos *(beginning on page 78)* depict the arrival of car 101 at Alton on the afternoon of October 17, 1952. In the time honored fashion, the car pulled into the station which was nestled in the shadow of the huge Occidental Flour mill silos. After picking up another load of passengers, pulling the pole and resetting the controls to the opposite end, the car rolls back southward towards St. Louis. A connection was made at this point with a railbus that took passengers on to Grafton.

GRANITE CITY LOCAL SERVICE

Eight PCC cars were placed into service from St. Louis Car Company in November 1949 in order to modernize the local streetcar service from St. Louis to Granite City. This was done a year after the Streamliners were purchased and would come to represent the very last effort by the Illinois Terminal to improve its image to the public, an effort that was soon proven to have been an exercise in futility. The IT became the very last US property to adopt the PCC car as a vehicle of choice. The Granite City operation would also become the last IT electrified operation, lasting some three years beyond the cessation of inter-city electric operation. The service ended on June 22, 1958, and two of the cars, 450 and 451 survive to this day in museums. The remainder of the PCC fleet was sold for scrap.

ABOVE AND BELOW • PCC 453 is seen taking the Adams Street curve on the Granite City loop on October 17, 1952. The same car is about to climb over one of the many railroad yards that permeated the cities of Venice, Madison, and Granite City following a spate of early 1950s vintage automobiles. These three locales were *(and still are)* a veritable sea of railroad yards. Because of the vulnerability of the freight cars to pilferage, these areas were frequented by the criminal element seeking to pilfer the freight from the cars and made photography a dangerous proposition, even in those seemingly innocent 1950's days. Nevertheless, our railfan brethren were committed to recording the scene on film, no matter what the price.

ABOVE • PCC car 451 is seen passing by the Granite City shops and yard complex. This facility provided a home for the entire Alton and Granite City local car fleet as well as numerous freight motors. Most of the maintenance on the interurban cars was performed at the Decatur shop. This photo was taken on October 6, 1950. Notice the protective glove covering the coupler. This was done to minimize corrosion on the electrical connecting pins on the coupler.

ABOVE • The 454 is seen from the rear as it entered the Granite City yard on October 6, 1950. The PCC cars were always maintained at this location. Of the more than 4,000 PCC cars constructed in the United States, only a very few were of this double-ended design. The "ice cream store" insert in the right hand windshield panel was to provide an escape hatch, should the car become disabled on one of the viaducts without a walkway.

ABOVE AND BELOW • The sun was definitely not cooperating when this shot was taken in the Granite City Yard on October 6, 1950. Prominently displayed are cars 121 and 407 spliced by a then fairly new PCC car. Another view of the overall yard and shop complex shows that the IT tended to segregate like cars on separate tracks for ease of dispatching.

STUDYING THE STREAMLINERS

In June 1948, the Illinois Terminal had its three sets of multi-car Streamliners under construction at the St. Louis Car Company, as well as the eight multiple-unit PCC cars. The Streamliners had been under design since 1945, and had been on order since 1946, when IT wartime riding had peaked at over 8 million passengers in one year. By 1948, however, passenger numbers had severely plummeted, but IT did not cancel the order, because their newest intercity rail equipment was already 30 years old. Moreover, their cars had been technologically obsolete for over 25 of those 30 years. No one could accurately predict what the future of rail passenger transportation would bode, but the prevailing attitude among the mid-western railroads in general was that, "if you build it, they will come." The Rock Island and the CB&Q, to name two, were into investing in streamliner equipment, with the RI serving the Chicago to Peoria route, while the CB&Q connecting Burlington with St. Louis, up and down the Mississippi River was also into lightweight streamliner equipment.

Whereas the Wabash Railroad offered superior service between Decatur and St. Louis, with over an hour shorter running time, there was no direct rail passenger train competition between Peoria and St. Louis. The IT opted to invest in streamlined three-car trains, with a parlor car bringing up the rear for this service. Two train sets would operate between Peoria and St. Louis, while a third train, minus the intermediate car in the center would operate from Decatur to St. Louis, joining the main line at Springfield. Van's 1948 visit to IT centered around brief visits to Alton, Springfield, Peoria and Decatur.

On October 21, 1948, an ill-fated clearance test run was performed using the first three-car train of Streamliners into the Peoria Terminal building. The designers' worst nightmares came true when the trains failed to clear the tight radius curves in the station area and the pilot struck the pavement at the bottom of the bridge ramp, known in the trade as a "vertical curve." This event doomed the operation of Streamliners into Peoria from the very outset.

November 7, 1948 would see the inauguration of the first scheduled Streamliner service between East Peoria and St. Louis. A 400-series streetcar was pressed into shuttle service over the Illinois River Bridge into Peoria, lasting about three months until the IT could secure permission to abandon the trackage and the bridge. The Streamliners were initially very prone to breakdowns and were shortly withdrawn from service and returned to the car builder for modifications. By January 1st, all service had reverted to the traditional two-car trains of heavyweight interurbans, with a combine being paired with a motorized trailer car. The ever-optimistic Illinois Terminal issued a timetable dated February 27, 1949 showing the Streamliners on the cover and touting the two round trips daily between the flagship cities. Full Streamliner service, however, was not offered until May of 1949.

ABOVE ● Car 300, a control cab with a motorman door, a baggage/express door and a passenger door is seen at East Peoria on October 2, 1950.

To build the Streamliners, St. Louis Car Company apparently drew heavily on the carbody designs that were used between 1934 and 1942 by ACF and EMC, not to mention their own 1941 plans for the North Shore Electroliners. The esthetics were also strongly influenced by the Budd-built Zephyrs on the CB&Q and Boston and Maine. The basic difference was that the IT cars were made of aluminum, whereas the others were mostly welded high-tensile steel in content. After nine months in service, the Streamliners already had a rather checkered history, and the parlor car seating was doomed to extinction.

ABOVE • In order to show the comparison of the Electroliner design with the IT Streamliner configuration, the author drew upon his own photo collection to show the similarities. This photo of a North Shore Electroliner was taken at Waukegan, Illinois on January 16, 1960. The Electroliners at that time were almost twenty years old, while the IT Streamliners had been sold for scrap at the age of six. *(Bill Volkmer)*

ABOVE • A three-car train presented a sort of "group photo" on October 5, 1950. Very soon thereafter, the parlor lounge cars were sidelined and the mighty Streamliners became ordinary coach-only venues with literally no esthetic value when viewed from the rear. On the next page we shall illustrate the individual car types as roster photos.

ABOVE AND BELOW • Car 331 was a motorized coach/trailer, containing a set of controls for hostling use only, very similar to the set-up on diesel "B" units that were coming into vogue on the Class 1 railroads at the time. Note that the trucks were placed as close to the end of the cars as physically possible. This was in deference to the sharp curves that the cars were required to negotiate in the city streets along the line. Trucks spaced at the normal intervals would have prohibited passengers from passing between the cars while the train was in motion. Car 350 was a parlor-lounge car, seating 33 people and had a bullet end. It carried a drum tail sign indicating the name of the train. The 350 was named the *Louis Jolliet:* after the early French explorer who civilized the Illinois River Valley. Whereas the French spelled "Joliet" with but one "L", the IT, for some unexplained reason, used two! A controller in the center of the rear vestibule allowed backup moves at Springfield and at turning wyes. There were loops at both East Peoria and St. Louis.

RIGHT • The formerly AC-powered right-of-way is captured as the blunted tail end of a Streamliner climbs Caldwell Hill on March 21, 1953. This stretch used Alternating Current only during a brief period after it was constructed and until DC rotating equipment could be installed. The right-of-way in this area was among the most well ballasted on the system, chiefly because of the pounding it took from heavy freights fighting their way up the grade.

ABOVE • A three-car Streamliner train featuring round-end parlor car FORT CREVECOUER prepares to leave Springfield on August 20, 1952. The wrong pole is up because of the stub-ended nature of the Springfield terminal track arrangement. Whereas formerly the IT operated through the city streets of Springfield, the trains now backed out of the station to a nearby wye, located on the belt line bypass trackage. There the crew changed ends and continued in forward motion to the destination city.

ABOVE • Car 302 is leading a three-car Streamliner out of Springfield as Train 93. On August 20, 1952, that train still had its parlor car, but not for long thereafter.

ABOVE ● On May 2, 1953 a southbound Streamliner was caught flying past Athol Tower on the north side of Lincoln. The track at this particular location was relocated to its present configuration in an effort to ease the curvature in the area for freight trains and speed up the operation in general. The tower controlled the Illinois Central as well as the Gulf, Mobile and Ohio in the general vicinity of both railroad stations. The IT station was located farther down in the center of town. The IC track is the one in the foreground.

ABOVE ● After passing Athol Tower, the blunt rear end was exposed for Van to photograph. The bullet end observation parlor car had been amputated in a cost-cutting move due to lack of patronage. The IT track paralleled the GM&O through Lincoln (population 14,000).

ABOVE ● Elkhart was hardly a fly-spec on the map, about 10 miles south of Lincoln, but the Streamliners stopped there nevertheless. At 12:18 on August 20, 1950, the two-car FORT CREVECOUR made the stop while running one car short of a full train. The Streamliners were trouble plagued during that period causing the trains to sometimes run short of a full complement of cars.

ABOVE ● A little later on during the Streamliner chase of May 2, 1953, Van caught up with the train at the town of Williamsville, six miles south of Elkhart.

LEFT ● One of the more photogenic spots from which to photograph the IT was the overpass just east of Starne Tower. A northbound Streamliner representing train 90 on August 20, 1950 is clattering over the frogs north of Springfield at 12:18 PM on its daily run to East Peoria from St. Louis.

RIGHT • In a somewhat classic pose, a short-lived three-car Streamliner train was photographed southbound crossing the long viaduct over the Gulf, Mobile, and Ohio Railroad south of Springfield on August 20, 1950. Van had to "strike while the iron was hot" because the Streamliners were initially trouble prone causing the three-car trains to either be truncated or have old cars substituted. Then no sooner did the IT get the Streamliners operational than they found that there was not enough patronage to sustain the parlor car, causing the trains to be shortened to two-cars and ultimately, one car. There is an old railfan adage that says, never take the present day scene for granted, because it will probably be gone tomorrow. That is what motivates the movement to preserve this type of history on film.

BELOW • A vintage Mobil Oil Company "flying red horse" sign stands sentry as a Streamliner, lead by car 300 pauses to take on passengers at Edwards and Washington Avenues in Granite City on October 17, 1953. The two-car train has just left the center of the street for some private right-of-way running.

LEFT • South of Springfield, a southbound Streamliner darts along straight as an arrow trackage just prior to ducking under a railroad bridge that provided Van Dusen a good vantage point on October 18, 1952. The year, 1952, marked the mid-point in the short life of the Streamliners.

LEFT • Class "D" electric locomotive 72 is approaching Ruth siding south of Girard on the Springfield-St. Louis main line on September 7, 1955. The freight consists of a mix of grain boxcars and coal hoppers, two of the basic commodities that originate along the lines of the Illinois Terminal. The GM&O main line is on the left and this site was once the location of a coal mine called "Green Ridge."

BELOW • Auto traffic was required to cope with behemoth freight trains in "beautiful downtown Lincoln, Ill." on March 22, 1953. Shortly after the electrification was abandoned this traffic was diverted onto Illinois Central R.R. nearby trackage.

FREIGHT SERVICE - THE MAIN LINE

GILLESPIE INTERLUDE

On October 18, 1952 Mr. Van Dusen toured the IT main line from St. Louis to Springfield, taking photos along the way. At Gillespie, 47 miles north of St. Louis, he encountered some interurban freight and passenger action. That action is presented on this page and the next.

ABOVE • An early morning freight train is northbound entering Gillespie hauled by a very dirty Class "D" motor, number 71. The unit still sports its original orange paint scheme, now almost 12 years old. The 71 had been rebuilt in 1940 from loco 1581 to the newer, heavier, more streamlined Class D configuration.

ABOVE • Moving up to Gillespie station, the same northbound freight train is observed threading its way along Main Street. The 50's vintage freight cars, the presence of a caboose and the absence of dense traffic on the street remind us of the way it once was, before trucks took over much of the freight delivery business. The siding branching off the main track also hint of the "door-to-door" service that the traction lines offered, whereas the steam roads seldom provided.

ABOVE • Just after the freight train clears the main into a siding north of Gillespie, a southbound interurban in the form of car 283 makes the stop in front of the station. In the time-honored fashion, the two processes are accomplished simultaneously, passengers load into the rear and parcels, mostly newspapers, are unloaded at the front. Since this is a Sunday, the newspapers are likely to be a little on the heavy side, and the unloading takes a little longer than usual.

ABOVE • The street running in towns like Hamel did little to speed up the progress of freight traffic on the Illinois Terminal. On the other hand, it did make for some interesting photos and street traffic deviations as the motorists dodged the oncoming behemoth freight trains. This scene was made at Hamel on May 2, 1953.

ABOVE ● Sawyerville was a small town 42 miles north of St. Louis on the line to Springfield. A freight train lead by C motor 1598 is taking the siding for a northbound passenger run on May 2, 1953. Notice that the compound catenary on the main line becomes simple trolley wire in the siding, which had a capacity of 40 cars. The paralleling railroad in the background belonged to the Chicago and North Western Ry. (Litchfield and Madison Div.).

ABOVE ● Van hurried ahead to again shoot the same freight train at Staunton. An abandoned branch line once connected with the main at this point. The 1598 was one of the heavier Class "C" motors (80 tons) built between 1924 and 1930. Five units of this series were subsequently rebuilt to Class "D" motors in the early 1940s by ballasting them out to almost 109 tons and giving them the streamlined shrouding. The presence of diesels on freights that month gave added impetus towards photographing as many electric freights as possible.

RIGHT • Class "D" freight motor 73 is at the Peoria and Eastern Railroad underpass near Mackinaw Junction with a southbound freight. This is the same freight that Van had shot in Morton, about seven miles north of Mackinaw. Noteworthy in this photo is that the main line trackage from Peoria to St. Louis had real stone ballast as compared with the two branches which only had cinders for ballast. This was probably in deference to both the heavier freight train activity and the higher speeds of the Streamliners et al.

BELOW • Class "C" motor number 1597 is a northbound here at Channing, north of Mindale on March 21, 1963. The main line here looks like a main line with good ballast and compound catenary. It is interesting to note that the IT reverted to simple trolley wire on the sidings located along the main line.

ABOVE AND BELOW • When not performing helper service on Caldwell Hill, Class B motor 1569, painted in the more modern green paint scheme, was utilized as a switcher in the East Peoria Yard. One such occasion was lensed on April 19, 1952. The photo below shows the same unit out on the line at Kerfoot siding, having just completed a trip helping a southbound freight on the hill. Van was shooting out the window of the 1203 that he was riding into East Peoria. Quite often the E. Peoria switcher would take a cut of cars south to Caldwell siding so the crew could get an "early quit" and not have to wait around to be the helper engine on the through freight.

Caldwell Hill presented some good photo opportunities for "down on" shots. Opportunities such as this are relatively rare in flat Illinois and other mid-western states. Motor 73 was groaning slowly up the grade approaching the "summit" on March 27, 1953. The McKinley construction crews must have done a bit of blasting to make that cut and thereby reduce the railroad gradient during the early part of the century when the line was built. This also was unusual for mid-western interurban construction.

ABOVE ● Van's 1950 Chevy didn't quite make it out of the photo when a freight train lead by Class D motor 72 rolled northbound into Springfield on August 20, 1950.

ABOVE ● The summer days were waning on September 7, 1955 and the weeds were growing well on the siding at South Carlinville when Class D motor 71 brought a southbound freight through the area. In less than a year diesels would take over the run and the overhead wires would be pulled down.

FREIGHT TO DANVILLE

ABOVE • The 1587 is lugging freight into a late afternoon sun in Champaign on May 15, 1954. Soon after passenger service was abandoned the freight traffic was given over to diesels, largely on trackage rights over paralleling "steam" roads.

ABOVE • It gets hot in the cab of an electric freight locomotive, even in April, in Illinois. On April 19, 1952, the 1583 paused in the siding at Muncie to await the arrival of a westbound passenger run.

DANVILLE POWER HOUSE

ABOVE • Motor 1554 was spotted at Granite City early on the morning of October 6, 1950. It apparently had been sent here for motor work, or wheel work. Ostensibly it was on leave of absence from its regular job, switching coal hoppers at the Danville Power House. It was built by the Danville Car Company in 1907 and rode on Baldwin trucks. The other locomotives in this series, 1553, 1555 to 1558 were all sold off in the 1930s to the Allis-Chalmers Company in Springfield which converted them to diesel-electrics. The early morning fog from the nearby Mississippi River shrouds this tired old veteran, making the photo somehow look like it was taken many years before.

ABOVE • Class A motor 1554 was still on active duty at the Danville Power Plant on August 18, 1951. It was used to shuffle coal hopper cars to and from the unloading point after an IT freight had set them off. The motor was off the roster of the IT and was the property of the Illinois-Iowa Power Company, owner of the plant.

ROSTER SHOTS

ABOVE • Combine 258 was found stored unserviceable in Decatur on June 19, 1948 sans headlight among other vital parts. These parts had no doubt been "stolen" by a shop hand to be put on another car undergoing overhaul, or by a light-fingered railfan with tools. In all probability, the car was serving as a parts supply to keep the other cars in service. This practice was typical of interurban companies during the 30s and 40s, struggling for their lives. The 258 was originally built in 1906 by the St. Louis Car Company as Mr. McKinley's private car *Indiana*. It measured 10 feet longer than the standard interurban cars of the era on the IT, which were then being delivered in the 225 series. The wooden car received steel sheathing in 1923 and it was scrapped on November 13, 1950, two years after this photo was made.

RIGHT, CENTER • Car 280 was built by St. Louis Car Company in 1913. It operated on the Chicago, Ottawa & Peoria Division until 1922 when it was reassigned to the main part of the system. It was converted to a parlor car *(Tangerine Flyer)* in 1924, the last year Bill McKinley was president of the road. Parlor seating was removed in 1929 and the car was scrapped in March 1956.

RIGHT • The 278 was one of a group of eleven similar cars built by St. Louis Car Co. in 1913. It was extensively rebuilt in 1919 during a standardization move on the IT. Five of this series, including the 278 received air-conditioning during the late 1930s. On April 19, 1952, it apparently was being used as the protect (i.e. backup) car at East Peoria for the Bloomington line, when the two remaining 1200-series cars, normally assigned the run, were down for repairs. The car has escaped the painter's gun, and would continue to do so through retirement. It apparently saw little revenue service after 1953. It was operated on the last day of the Bloomington line and was scrapped two years later, on May 19, 1954.

RIGHT • Car 270 was originally built as the parlor car *Glenna* for the Columbus, Delaware and Marion Ry. Company in Ohio by the Niles Car Company, in March 1907. It was only on that property a short time when it was resold to the Illinois Traction System and was used as their parlor car *Bloomington*. The IT stripped the car of its parlor car seating, along with sister car 271 in February 1922, and at 68' 6" in length, made them the longest coaches on the railroad. As coaches, they seated 47, and were retired on April 9, 1951 and June 3, 1952 respectively.

RIGHT • Trailer 530 looked to be in pretty decent shape while it was on a fantrip at Springfield on May 2, 1953. There were still six of them on the roster as of this date and three of the six were at Springfield this date.

BELOW • Trailer cars 530 and 531 were the only two to get the black-stripe-down-the-side paint treatment. The 531 kept that scheme, but the 530 was repainted into the blue scheme when it passed through the Decatur shops in the early 1950s. It was built in 1912 and retired on April 19, 1956. Later it was utilized as a yard office in Springfield's East Belt Yards. The body was finally sold to a private individual in 1972. It was photographed here in Springfield on May 2, 1953.

ABOVE • One of the last remaining wooden express trailers, number 606 (series 604-607) was seen at East Peoria yard on April 19, 1952. It was one of a group of four express trailers converted from freight motors 1063-1067. The 606 was originally built as an express motor in 1910 by the McGuire Cummings Car Company and was demotorized in February 1935. It became a passenger trailer for the war effort on May 15, 1942 to haul workers to a munitions plant in Illiopolis. As car 560, it contained four large benches. After the war, in March 1947, it reverted to an express trailer, and the benches were removed. It was finally scrapped at Granite City on January 20, 1956.

RIGHT • The Illinois Terminal purchased four freight/express motor cars from the Cincinnati and Lake Erie when that line went out of business in the late 1930s. IT never used them as powered cars, even though they were less than 10 years old at the time of purchase, and were some of the last interurban freight motors ever constructed. Car 603 is shown here at Springfield on April 20, 1952. The conversion to the blue paint scheme indicates that the car was on the list of "keepers" at that time.

RIGHT • Originally constructed as an open observation reserved seat trailer coach/parlor, the 512's observation deck was closed in during a 1936 rebuilding. It underwent a mini-rehab in 1951 and was painted in the blue livery to substitute for the ailing Streamliners in what was locally referred to as "The Blue Train". It was photographed at the Decatur Shops on September 29, 1951. At that time all of its team-mates, 510-511, and 513-515 had been retired and scrapped, most of them in 1950. Unfortunately the blue paint didn't exactly prolong the life of this car either, for it was sold for scrap less than a year later, August 26, 1952.

ABOVE • Motorized trailer 531 is seen at Springfield on May 31, 1953. It was built in 1912 and survived to the end of passenger service, being scrapped in September 1956.

ABOVE AND BELOW • Motorized trailer 516 has never had its arch-windows covered over indicating that it was never modernized in the 1940 rebuilding program. It was sold for scrap on November 13, 1950. It was photographed at Springfield station on June 18, 1948. Compare this photo with the 526, taken the same day. The 526 was modernized. It met its fate on July 16, 1951.

ABOVE AND BELOW • Two views of IT 404 are presented here. The photo was made on October 6, 1950 while it was passing by the Granite City yards on Madison Avenue. The photo was made two years later, on October 17, 1952. The car was built by St. Louis Car in 1924, one of a group of 12 (404-415) similar lightweight interurban cars for the Illinois Valley Division of ITS. Original numbers were 60-64, 68, and 70-71, 73-76. They were renumbered in 1930 when they were moved over to the IT main routes. 404 was originally numbered 60, but carried number 74 after the first 74 was in a wreck in 1928. For some inexplicable reason, these cars were built with arched windows, during an era long past the time when arch windows were in fashion. The upper window sashes on all IT cars were sheathed over during the late 1930s primarily to cut down the amount of sunlight encountered by the air-conditioning systems on the interurban coaches.

LEFT • Car 121 was one of a group of four cars (120-123) that were originally built for the East St. Louis and Suburban Railway in that company's shops in May 1924 for service on the local streetcar system in the East St. Louis area. Originally numbered 4, 5, 11, and 15 on the ESL&S, they were renumbered in August 1931 to the 120-series and deeded over to the Illinois Terminal for Alton line service. Seating 58, they were retired on July 23, 1953 and sold for scrap.

ABOVE • St. Louis Car Company built an order of four cars for the St. Louis and Alton Railroad in 1924. The multiple-unit center-entrance cars were very modern for their time when compared with other cars being offered at the time. Most of the time, the foursome ran in two two-car trains, but occasionally they ventured out as single units. The 470 is shown here at the Granite City. They survived about six years after retirement, being sold for scrap on July 24, 1959. On the SL&A they were numbered 70-73, but had to be renumbered because of the conflict with the freight motors.

CENTER AND BOTTOM • Streamliner 301 is seen at Springfield Station on April 20, 1952. Compare this photo with the North Shore Electroliner taken March 3, 1951. The IT car is aluminum, the North Shore car is made of high tensile steel. The IT car has skirts, while the North Shore car does not. The reason the North Shore avoided skirts was undoubtedly to allow easier access to the car's underside in third rail territory.

(Bottom, Bill Volkmer Collection)

THE "PULL" CARS

ABOVE • Car 1202 along with a companion express trailer was at E. Peoria on May 19, 1952. The IT combines were rather unique in that, they were single end and had the express door only on the right-hand side of the car. There was a small door at the corner of the left hand side for the crew to have access to the cab without negotiating the baggage compartment inside. Four cars, 1200-1203 were built in December 1910 to carry mail on the Hillsboro Branch and to tow the sleepers from Peoria to St. Louis. As built, the cars had a radically different appearance, with large express compartments and seating in the rear for only 24 people.

In 1921, the four cars were extensively rebuilt to the configuration shown on this page.

ABOVE • Car 1203, having lost its regular job on the Bloomington line in February 1953, has become an "extra" on call at Springfield, on May 2, 1953. It is mated with the 531.

CLASS B MOTORS

ABOVE • Still almost pristine in its traction orange paint scheme, 1576 seems to have escaped the paint brush because it still seems to be advertising War Bonds, unless this was a holdover from the Korean War. The photo was taken at the Granite City Shops on May 3, 1953.

ABOVE • Class "B" motor 1568, a product of the Illinois Terminal's Decatur Shop, one of 18 units constructed between 1910 and 1918. It was spotted at Springfield yard on June 18, 1948. Number 1565 of this class is preserved at the Illinois Railway Museum in Union, Ill.

CLASS C MOTORS

ABOVE • Class "C" freight motor 1582 was one of 20 similar locomotives built in the Decatur Shop between 1924 and 1930. It was apparently being held at E. Peoria as a protect engine when photographed on April 19, 1952. The two large canisters on the pilot displaying the road numbers were sand boxes.

ABOVE • Sister locomotive 1586 on June 19, 1948 still wore the original dark green livery that was applied to all passenger equipment prior to the mid-1920s era rebuilding and repainting to the tangerine colors.

LEFT • Loco 1579 was the first of the class of 1924 heavyweight C motors to be turned out of the Decatur Shops. Unlike the 1586 above, the unit apparently made it back into the paint shop in recent years to receive the last style green paint scheme applied. It was seen with a brakeman riding the footboards on August 31, 1955. Alas, locomotives no longer are allowed to have footboards in interchange service.

CLASS D MOTORS

ABOVE • Class "D" streamlined freight locomotive 72, still in its original orange paint job, was seen at Springfield on August 20, 1950. The third of three such locomotives, it was built in 1942 during the early stages of World War II. Because of their photogenic qualities, the Class "D"s tended to appear in all IT promotional literature pertaining to freight services.

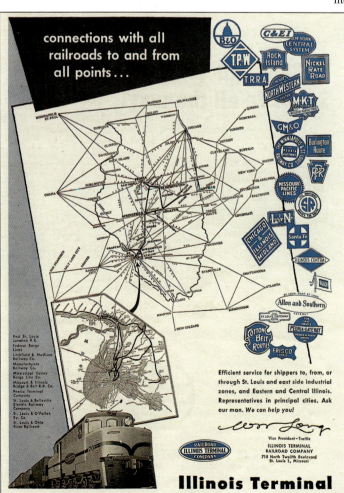

ABOVE • Number 51 was a battery-equipped diesel-electric/straight-electric locomotive built as a tri-power demonstrator by the St. Louis Car Company in 1930. During that time, steam roads were looking for alternatives to steam in the form of gasoline, diesel and hybrid electric locomotives such as this. The unit was one of two built at the time, 52 being the other loco. They were used almost exclusively in the St. Louis to Alton area, principally because of weight restrictions over the McKinley Bridge into St. Louis. The delivery of Alco diesel switchers and roadswitchers in 1948 limited their usefulness.

HYBRID ELECTRIC LOCOMOTIVES

ABOVE • Locomotive 53 was built in 1941 as a sister to the 51 and 52 that had been delivered to the IT a decade earlier. It did not include the battery pack that 51 and 52 were equipped with. It was built in the Decatur Shop at about the same time as the heavy duty Class "D" locos were built.

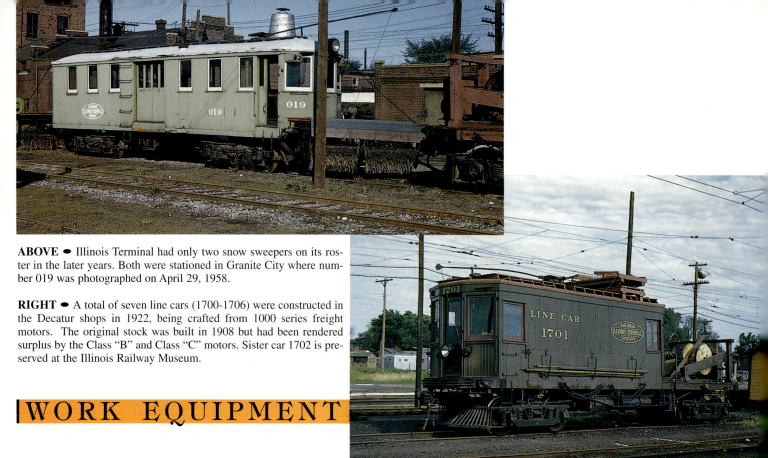

ABOVE • Illinois Terminal had only two snow sweepers on its roster in the later years. Both were stationed in Granite City where number 019 was photographed on April 29, 1958.

RIGHT • A total of seven line cars (1700-1706) were constructed in the Decatur shops in 1922, being crafted from 1000 series freight motors. The original stock was built in 1908 but had been rendered surplus by the Class "B" and Class "C" motors. Sister car 1702 is preserved at the Illinois Railway Museum.

WORK EQUIPMENT

ABOVE • Bunk car 098 began life as a trailer coach, 527, from St. Louis Car Company in September 1911. In 1930 it was converted to the bedroom car ILLINOIS and carried number 501. Twelve years later, in 1942, it was re-converted to a trailer, this time numbered 535, to handle wartime loads. Then on September 18, 1952, it became bunk car 098. On March 21, 1953 it had its picture taken here at Mindale station and on August 22, 1966, it was sold to a private individual in Harristown, Ill.

LEFT • Portable substation 056 was at Mindale station on March 21, 1953. At that time it was pinch hitting for the permanent machinery at that locale, which was apparently down for extensive repairs. The workers bunked out in bunk car 098, that was parked next door for the duration. Being portable, the unit was later transferred to Ogden, on the Danville line, after the line east of DeLong was abandoned leaving that area without a permanent substation.

Box car 6056, a 50-foot, single-door car was in general freight service when snapped in Phoenix, Arizona on September 1, 1973. During that period of time it was fashionable for shortlines everywhere to be in the freight car rental business as an additional source of revenue.

FREIGHT CARS

Whereas Gordon Lloyd's book contained several fine examples of Illinois Terminal freight rolling stock, Gene Van Dusen was not big on taking photographs of freight cars. There were, however, a couple of slides in his collection that were worthy of reproduction here, hence they are presented. For a more in-depth look at the IT freight car fleet, the reader is encouraged to consult Volume I of this series.

ABOVE • This fairly new caboose had been minted the previous year by the St. Louis Car Company. It was seen here at Decatur Shops on May 15, 1954. Naturally it long outlived the era of the electric interurban on the ITS until the caboose as an institution went the way of the interurban in the 1970s.

THE DIESEL ERA

The IT received their first commercially built diesels in 1948, in the form of 12 Alco S-2 switchers and six Alco RS-1 roadswitchers numbered 751-756 delivered the same year. These units replaced all steam power in the Alton-Granite City area. The freight fleet in 1949 consisted of 45 electric locomotives, 18 diesels, and 1,939 freight cars. After the electrification ended, various additions were made to the diesel fleet.

ABOVE • Long after electric locomotives had ceased to haul freight out of East Peoria, this trio of units lead by IT 2004, a GP-38-2, was spotted at Allentown Yard. The 2004 was one of four GP-38-2s purchased new from EMD in 1977. The date was April 4, 1981 and the third unit in the consist belonged to Conrail. The Illinois Terminal tracks from Allentown to Lincoln had been abandoned since August 6, 1977. *(Kenneth L. Douglas, Bill Volkmer collection)*

LEFT • Earlier in this book we witnessed an electric freight motor pulling into the Sawyerville Siding for a meet on May 2, 1953. That meet was made by one of the IT GP-7s that had been recently delivered to the road from La Grange. Because the diesels were considered to be too heavy for the lightweight rail in the sidings, the alert dispatcher had to program the meets so that diesels did not pass one another and when a diesel passed an electric, the diesel kept to the main track.

LEFT • Because of weight restrictions into St. Louis, the small Alco S-2 1000 HP switchers were kept in that area, along with the former battery/electric locomotives. Alco 710 was idling away the time in the St. Louis subway area on September 7, 1953. Under the structure, in the background, is one of the ex-Cincinnati and Lake Erie trailers, probably being loaded with bread from a nearby bakery.

ABOVE • A two unit GP-39-2 set makes a set-off at Springfield's East Belt Yard on June 26, 1977. *(M. Wise, Bill Volkmer collection)*

ABOVE • The Illinois Terminal inherited some rebuilt cast-off GP-10s from locomotive rebuilders. One such unit was 1750. The date was January 1972. *(Bill Volkmer Collection)*

IT CARS IN MUSEUMS

ABOVE • The first car to be preserved by a museum was a true gem. Car 241 is pictured here at the St. Louis Museum of Transport, west of St. Louis on October 5, 1950 in bad need of a new paint job. It had been officially retired on June 1, 1950. The car was one of five cars originally equipped for AC operation between Peoria and Springfield. Five other cars (245-249) were built at the same time as DC cars by the American Car and Foundry in May 1908. The AC experiment was very short lived and all 10 remained in service until they were gradually retired beginning in 1936. Car 248 of the series proved to be the "survivor", staying on the roster until 1952 and carrying the distinction of never having lost its graceful arched window configuration to the modernization process.

ABOVE • The sleeping car *Peoria* a.k.a. 534 and later work car 049 has been restored at the Illinois Railway Museum. The photo is dated September 24, 1976.

RIGHT AND BELOW • Car 233 was preserved by the Illini Railroad Club in Champaign because it was originally the McKinley private car *Missouri*. The car had been destroyed in a head-on collision at DeLong on May 31, 1928 and was rebuilt into an office car. It was photographed in 1962 while it still resided in Champaign. In later years the car was moved to the Illinois Railway Museum where it re-joined its former team mate 234 shown (below) at the IRM on September 1, 1973. The two cars were painted blue early in the 1950 era repainting program and toured the system as a two-car train of company officers' private cars. The 234 had always retained its original appearance as an open-platformed observation car.

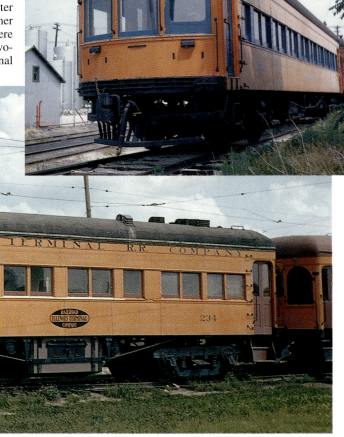

ILLINOIS 120 TERMINAL

OHIO RAILWAY MUSEUM

ABOVE • Two IT PCC cars were saved out of the eight. The 450 was preserved at the Ohio Railway Museum in Worthington, Ohio where it was photographed by the author on October 17, 1971. *(Bill Volkmer)*

BELOW • The 451 pictured was saved at the Connecticut Electric Railway Museum at Warehouse Point, Connecticut. In the early 1980s both preserved PCC cars were loaned for a period of almost three years to the Shaker Heights Rapid Transit in Cleveland because of a shortage of cars. *(Bill Volkmer collection)*

FANTRIPS

Railfan excursions played a huge role in making the Illinois Terminal photographically accessible during the final years of operation. Many of the photos in this book would not have been possible were it not for these excursions. The reason is simple. When there were only one or two trips made each day, a would-be photographer might only be able to catch a photo at, say, one location on the entire run, because it was just not possible to drive faster than the subject was traveling in order to get set up for additional photos. In the early 1950s, there were no Interstate Highways and each and every U.S. highway, including the now infamous Route 66, went straight through the center of each and every town and city. Bypasses were common around medium and large cities in the eastern United States but were rare indeed in Illinois.

During the execution of the railfan excursions, every effort was made to exclude other photographers from the photo but inevitably, there were situations were there was no choice but to include other photographers. Because some of the locations showing photographers were not otherwise represented in this book, we are including a sampling of these photos here. Were it not for the noble souls pictured here, the history of electric traction would be much poorer in available quantity and quality.

ABOVE • During a brief period of overcast skies early on September 19, 1954, a four-car train of heavyweights was stopped in Gillespie for a photo opportunity.

BELOW • Later in the day, a diesel roadswitcher had towed the four car special over non-electrified trackage in the Alton area. They stopped at the coaling tower in Federal, Ill. for a photo before proceeding back towards Decatur and Danville. One of the cars in the special train was dropped off at this point to be placed into revenue service, towed by a diesel, while the remaining three continued on as a special.

ABOVE • A layover was held at the Decatur Shop for the fans to inspect whatever equipment might be lying around.

BELOW • The September 19, 1954 special train pictured on the previous page meets a regular car 284 at Bondville, between Decatur and Champaign.

LAST RUN TO DANVILLE

LEFT • The last run special on the Danville line on April 19, 1952 used the 285, which was a regular on the line at the time. It was the last heavyweight car built by and for the Illinois Terminal and was probably in better mechanical shape than most thanks to several rebuildings. This photo shows the fans swarming the car at a stop westbound near DeLong, a point that would soon be the truncated end of the Danville line.

BELOW • Trailer 532 is bringing up the rear of a two-car special on April 20, 1952 as the special returns to Danville. The IT crossed over the Chicago and Eastern Illinois mainline here at Glover tower. The C&EI line connected Chicago with Evansville, Indiana and later became a branch of the Louisville and Nashville R.R.

ABOVE • Car 285 that had been the chartered car the day before has been returned to regular service and the Sunday special made a meet with it at Monticello. Even though many of the cars were saved for museums and posterity, both the 285 and 532 would be scrapped after service was discontinued over the railroad.

ABOVE • An Illini Railroad Club fantrip on May 3, 1953 produced this very nice shot of the two-car special consisting of combine 276 and trailer 530 at Champaign station westbound. The New York Central station for the same city was on the opposite side of the track.

THE ILLINOIS TERMINAL RE-INCARNATED

The preponderance of this book consists of photographs taken by one person, Eugene Van Dusen. A small number were taken by Gene at the Illinois Railway Museum and appear earlier in the book. However, the author felt that the book might be more complete if a selection of photos, taken from his own collection, were posted in order to illustrate what a marvelous job the members of IRM are doing to recreate the ambiance that the original IT possessed. Take a look for yourself.

LEFT • Nicely appointed combine 277 with a trailer on 10-15-83. The 277 carried the distinction of being the last revenue passenger car in operation on the Illinois Terminal.
(D.F. Burnette, Volkmer Collection)

LEFT • Motorized trailer car 518 is seen at the IRM on May 27, 1978.
(Bill Volkmer collection)

LEFT • 277, 518, Peoria, 234 September 18, 1976 *(Bill Volkmer collection)*

BELOW • Four-car train being operated on September 18, 1976. This represents a re-creation of a typical Illinois Terminal sleeper train from Peoria to St. Louis, a service that had been discontinued for 36 years.
(Bill Volkmer collection)

ABOVE • Former St. Louis and Alton Electric 101 at the IRM on May 30, 1988. *(Eugene Van Dusen)*

RIGHT • Car 101 holds down the regular run on the IRM trackage on October 2, 1993. *(Bob Townley)*

BELOW • Car 415, former Illinois Valley Division lightweight suburban car at IRM on October 30, 1988. This car is literally the workhorse of the museum. *(Bill Volkmer collection)*

ABOVE • Line Car 1702 on April 4, 1959.
(Eugene Van Dusen)

RIGHT • Class "B" locomotive 1565 at IRM in October 1969.
(Karl Henkels, Bill Volkmer collection)

RIGHT • Class "B" freight locomotive 1565 at IRM in June 1977. *(Bill Volkmer collection)*

FINAL FRAME

ABOVE • In preparing this book for publication, we have tried to recreate the ambiance and feeling that WAS the interurban era, through the medium of photographs. As a final offering, we would like to pay tribute to the folks at the Illinois Railway Museum for their part in *completely* re-creating that atmosphere in real time. The persons responsible for this are to be commended not only for the results of their effort, but for the fact that they are volunteering their time and monetary resources to do so. There is an entire new generation of people here today who not only never saw an interurban in action, but generally are not aware that the institution ever existed in the first place. This exhibit and others like it are living history, not just a static display and it is hoped that the memory of the Illinois Terminal Railroad and others are kept alive long after those of us who photographically and physically attempted to preserve it have passed on.